L-00

William Shakespeare's
KING LEAR

W9-BMP-204

Robert Schuettinger
Earhart Fellow
Oxford University

Copyright © 1997, 1965 by Simon & Schuster, Inc.

This edition published by Barnes & Noble, Inc.,
by arrangement with Macmillan Publishing USA,
a division of Simon & Schuster, Inc.

All rights reserved. No part of this book
may be used or reproduced in any manner whatsoever
without the written permission of the Publisher.

1997 Barnes & Noble Books

MACMILLAN is a registered trademark of Macmillan, Inc.
Monarch and colophons are trademarks of Simon & Schuster, Inc.,
registered in the U.S. Patent and Trademark Office.

Macmillan Publishing USA
A division of Simon & Schuster, Inc.
1633 Broadway
New York, NY   10019

ISBN 0-7607-0571-2

Text design by Tony Meisel

Printed and bound in the United States of America.

99 00 01 M 9 8 7 6 5 4 3

RRDC

CONTENTS

INTRODUCTION

FACTS VERSUS SPECULATION

Anyone who wishes to know where documented truth ends and where speculation begins in Shakespearean scholarship and criticism first needs to know the facts of Shakespeare's life. A medley of life records suggest, by their lack of inwardness, how little is known of Shakespeare's ideology, his beliefs and opinions.

William Shakespeare was baptized on April 26, 1564, as "Gulielmus filius Johannes Shakspere"; the evidence is the parish register of Holy Trinity Church, Stratford, England.

HUSBAND AND FATHER

On November 28, 1582, the Bishop of Worcester issued a license to William Shakespeare and "Anne Hathwey of Stratford" to solemnize a marriage upon one asking of the banns providing that there were no legal impediments. Three askings of the banns were (and are) usual in the Church of England.

On May 26, 1583, the records of the parish church in Stratford note the baptism of Susanna, daughter to William Shakespeare. The inference is clear, then, that Anne Hathaway Shakespeare was with child at the time of her wedding.

On February 2, 1585, the records of the parish church in Stratford note the baptisms of "Hamnet & Judeth, sonne and daughter to William Shakspere."

SHAKESPEARE INSULTED

On September 20, 1592, Robert Greene's *A Groats-worth of witte, bought with a million of Repentance* was entered in the Stationers' Register. In this work Shakespeare was publicly insulted as "an upstart Crow, beautified with our ["gentlemen" playwrights usually identified as Marlowe, Nashe, and Lodge] feathers, that with Tygers hart wrapt in a Players hyde [a parody of a Shakespearean line in II Henry VI] supposes he is as well able to bombast out a blank verse as the best of you: and being an absolute Iohannes fac totum, is in his own conceit the only Shake-scene in a country." This statement asperses not only Shakespeare's art but intimates his base, i.e., nongentle, birth. A "John factotum" is a servant or a man of all work.

On April 18, 1593, Shakespeare's long erotic poem "Venus and Adonis" was entered for publication. It was printed under the author's name and was dedicated to the nineteen-year-old Henry Wriothesley, Earl of Southampton.

On May 9, 1594, another long erotic poem, "The Rape of Lucrece," was entered for publication. It also was printed under Shakespeare's name and was dedicated again to the Earl of Southampton.

On December 26 and 27, 1594, payment was made to Shakespeare and others for performances at court by the Lord Chamberlain's servants.

For August 11, 1596, the parish register of Holy Trinity Church records the burial of "Hamnet filius William Shakspere."

FROM "VILLEIN" TO "GENTLEMAN"
On October 20, 1596, John Shakespeare, the poet's father, was made a "gentleman" by being granted the privilege of bearing a coat of arms. Thus, William Shakespeare on this day also became a "gentleman." Shakespeare's mother, Mary Arden Shakespeare, was "gentle" by birth. The poet was a product of a cross-class marriage. Both the father and the son were technically "villeins" or "villains" until this significant day.

On May 24, 1597, William Shakespeare purchased New Place, a large house in the center of Stratford.

CITED AS "BEST"

In 1598 Francis Meres's Palladis Tamia listed Shakespeare more frequently than any other English author. Shakespeare was cited as one of eight by whom "the English tongue is mightily enriched, and gorgeouslie invested in rare ornaments and resplendent abiliments"; as one of six who had raised *monumentum aere perennius* [a monument more lasting than brass]; as one of five who excelled in lyric poetry; as one of thirteen "best for Tragedie," and as one of seventeen who were "best for Comedy."

On September 20, 1598, Shakespeare is said on the authority of Ben Jonson (in his collection of plays, 1616) to have been an actor in Jonson's *Every Man in His Humour*.

On September 8, 1601, the parish register of Holy Trinity in Stratford records the burial of "Mr. Johannes Shakespeare," the poet's father.

BECOMES A "KING'S MAN"

In 1603 Shakespeare was named among others, the Lord Chamberlain's players, as licensed by James I (Queen Elizabeth having died) to become the King's Men.

In 1603 a garbled and pirated *Hamlet* (now known as Q1) was printed with Shakespeare's name on the title page.

In March 1604, King James gave Shakespeare, as one of the Grooms of the Chamber (by virtue of being one of the King's Men), four yards of red cloth for a livery, this being in connection with a royal progress through the City of London.

In 1604 (probably) there appeared a second version of *Hamlet* (now known as Q2), enlarged and corrected, with Shakespeare's name on the title page.

On June 5, 1607, the parish register at Stratford records the marriage of "M. John Hall gentleman & Susanna Shaxspere," the poet's elder daughter. John Hall was a doctor of medicine.

BECOMES A GRANDFATHER

On February 21, 1608, the parish register at Holy Trinity, Stratford, records the baptism of Elizabeth Hall, Shakespeare's first grandchild.

On September 9, 1608, the parish register at Holy Trinity, Stratford, records the burial of Mary Shakespeare, the poet's mother.

On May 20, 1609, "Shakespeares Sonnets. Never before Imprinted" was entered for publication.

On February 10, 1616, the marriage of Judith, Shakespeare's younger daughter, is recorded in the parish register of Holy Trinity, Stratford.

On March 25, 1616, Shakespeare made his will. It is extant.

On April 23, 1616, Shakespeare died. The monument in the Stratford church is authority for the date.

BURIED IN STRATFORD CHURCH

On April 25, 1616, Shakespeare was buried in Holy Trinity Church, Stratford. Evidence of this date is found in the church register. A stone laid over his grave bears the inscription:

Good Frend for Iesus Sake Forbeare, To Digg The Dust Encloased Heare! Blest Be The Man That Spares Thes Stones, And Curst Be He That Moves My Bones.

DEMAND FOR MORE INFORMATION

These are the life records of Shakespeare. Biographers, intent on book length or even short accounts of the life of the poet, of necessity flesh out these (and other) not very revealing notices from 1564 to 1616, Shakespeare's life span, with ancillary matter such as the status of Elizabethan actors, details of the Elizabethan theaters, and life under Elizabeth I and James I. Information about Shakespeare's artistic life—for example, his alteration of his sources—is much more abundant than truthful insights into his personal life, including his beliefs. There is, of course, great demand for colorful stories about Shakespeare, and there is intense pressure on biographers to depict the poet as a paragon of wisdom.

ANECDOTES—TRUE OR UNTRUE?
Biographers of Shakespeare may include stories about Shakespeare that have been circulating since at least the seventeenth century; no one knows whether or not these stories are true. One declares that Shakespeare was an apprentice to a butcher, that he ran away from his master, and was received by actors in London. Another story holds that Shakespeare was, in his youth, a schoolmaster somewhere in the country. Another story has Shakespeare fleeing from his native town to escape the clutches of Sir Thomas Lucy, who had often had him whipped and sometimes imprisoned for poaching deer. Yet another story represents the youthful Shakespeare as holding horses and taking care of them while their owners attended the theater. And there are other stories.

Scholarly and certainly lay expectations oblige Shakespearean biographers often to resort to speculation. This may be very well if biographers use such words as conjecture, presumably, seems, and almost certainly. I quote an example of this kind of hedged thought and language from Hazelton Spencer's *The Art and Life of William Shakespeare* (1940): "Of politics Shakespeare seems to have steered clear . . . but at least by implication Shakespeare reportedly endorses the strong-monarchy policy of the Tudors and Stuarts." Or one may say, as I do in my book *Blood Will Tell in Shakespeare's Plays* (1984): "Shakespeare particularly faults his numerous villeins for lacking the classical virtue of courage (they are cowards) and for deficiencies in reasoning ability (they are 'fools'), and in speech (they commit malapropisms), for lack of charity, for ambition, for unsightly faces and poor physiques, for their smell, and for their harboring lice." This remark is not necessarily biographical or reflective of Shakespeare's personal beliefs; it refers to Shakespeare's art in that it makes general assertions about the base—those who lacked coats of arms—as they appear in the poet's thirty-seven plays. The remark's truth or lack of truth may be tested by examination of Shakespeare's writings.

WHO WROTE SHAKESPEARE'S PLAYS?

The less reputable biographers of Shakespeare, including some of weighty names, state assumptions as if they were facts concerning the poet's beliefs. Perhaps the most egregious are those who cannot conceive that the Shakespearean plays were written by a person not a graduate of Oxford or Cambridge and destitute of the insights permitted by foreign travel and by life at court. Those of this persuasion insist that the seventeenth Earl of Oxford, Edward de Vere (whose descendant Charles Vere recently spoke up for the Earl's authorship of the Shakespearean plays), or Sir Francis Bacon, or someone else wrote the Shakespearean plays. It is also argued that the stigma of publication would besmirch the honor of an Elizabethan gentleman who published under his own name (unless he could pretend to correct a pirated printing of his writings).

BEN JONSON KNEW HIM WELL

Suffice it here to say that the thought of anyone writing the plays and giving them to the world in the name of Shakespeare would have astonished Ben Jonson, a friend of the poet, who literally praised Shakespeare to the skies for his comedies and tragedies in the fine poem "To the Memory of My Beloved Master the Author, Mr. William Shakespeare, and What He Hath Left Us" (printed in the First Folio, 1623). Much more commonplace and therefore much more obtrusive upon the minds of Shakespeare students are those many scholars who are capable of writing, for example, that Shakespeare put more of himself into Hamlet than any of his other characters or that the poet had no rigid system of religion or morality. Even George Lyman Kittredge, the greatest American Shakespearean, wrote, "Hamlet's advice to the players has always been understood—and rightly—to embody Shakespeare's own views on the art of acting."

In point of fact, we know nothing of Shakespeare's beliefs or opinions except such obvious inferences as that he must have thought New Place, Stratford, worth buying because he bought it. Even Homer, a very self-effacing poet, differs in this matter from Shakespeare. Twice in the *Iliad* he speaks in his own voice (distinguished from the dialogue of his characters) about certain evil deeds of Achilles. Shakespeare left no letters, no diary, and no prefaces (not counting conventionally obsequious dedications); no Elizabethan Boswell tagged Shakespeare around London and the provinces to record his conversations and thus to reveal his mind. In his plays Shakespeare employed no rainsonneur, or authorial mouthpiece, as some other dramatists have done: Contrary to many scholarly assertions, it cannot be proved that Prospero, in *The Tempest* in the speech ending "I'll drown my book" (Act V), and Ulysses, in *Troilus and Cressida* in the long speech on "degree" (Act II), speak Shakespeare's own sentiments. The characters in all Shakespearean plays speak for themselves. Whether they speak also for Shakespeare cannot be proved because documents outside the plays cannot be produced.

As for the sonnets, they have long been the happy hunting ground of biographical crackpots who lack outside documents, who do not recognize that Shakespeare may have been using a persona, and who seem not to know that in Shakespeare's time good sonnets were supposed to read like confessions.

Some critics even go to the length of professing to hear Shakespeare speaking in the speech of a character and uttering his private beliefs. An example may be found in A. L. Rowse's *What Shakespeare Read and Thought* (1981): "Nor is it so difficult to know what Shakespeare thought or felt. A writer, Logan Pearsall Smith, had the perception to see that a personal tone of voice enters when Shakespeare is telling you what he thinks, sometimes almost a raised voice; it is more obvious again when he urges the same point over and over."

BUT THERE'S NO PROOF!

Rowse, deeply enamoured of his ability to hear Shakespeare's own thoughts in the speeches of characters speaking in character, published a volume entitled *Shakespeare's Self-Portrait, Passages from His Work* (1984). One critic might hear Shakespeare voicing his own thoughts in a speech in *Hamlet;* another might hear the author in *Macbeth.* Shakespearean writings can become a vast whispering gallery where Shakespeare himself is heard here and everywhere, without an atom of documentary proof.

"BETTER SO"

Closer to truth is Matthew Arnold's poem on Shakespeare:

> Others abide our question. Thou art free.
> We ask and ask— thou smilest and art still,
> Out-topping knowledge. For the loftiest hill,
> Who to the stars uncrowns his majesty,
>
> Planting his steadfast footsteps in the sea,
> Making the heaven of heavens his dwelling-places,
> Spares but the cloudy border of his base
> To the foiled searching of mortality;
>
> And thou, who didst the stars and sunbeams know,
> Self-schooled, self-scanned, self-honoured, self-secure,
> Didst tread the earth unguessed at.— Better so. . . .

Here Arnold has Dichtung und Wahrheit—both poetry and truth—with at least two abatements: He exaggerates

Shakespeare's wisdom (the poet, after all, is not God); and Arnold fails to acknowledge that Shakespeare's genius was variously recognized in his own time. Jonson, for example, recorded that the "players [actors of the poet's time] have often mentioned it as an honor to Shakespeare, that in his writing (whatsoever he penned) he never blotted a line" (Timber). And of course there is praise of Shakespeare, some of it quoted above, in Meres's *Palladis Tamia* (1598).

THE BEST APPROACH

Hippocrates' first apothegm states, "Art is long, but life is short." Even Solomon complained of too many books. It is important to be selective. Certainly, we should study Shakespeare's very words, even memorize some of the more significant passages. Then, if we have time, we should turn to the golden insights of criticism from the eighteenth century to the present. However, the reader just getting acquainted with Shakespeare's works should be aware that among this body of criticism there is much that is repetitious, obvious, and subjective.

Time allowing, we might study the primary sources of Shakespeare's era because the plays naturally take on the coloration of their historical period. Finally, readers who wish to dig a bit deeper should read the works of biographers of Shakespeare who distinguish between fact and guesswork, such as Marchette Chute (*Shakespeare of London*). The happiest situation, pointed to by Jesus in Milton's *Paradise Regained,* is to bring judgment informed by knowledge to a study of Shakespeare's art.

KING LEAR
INTRODUCTION

BRIEF SUMMARY OF KING LEAR

King Lear is the ruler of pre-Christian Britain. He is a vigorous, sensitive man in his eighties who, because of long years of ruling, expects absolute devotion from all his subjects, especially his three daughters, Goneril, Regan and Cordelia. When the play begins, he has decided to abdicate his throne and divide Britain in equal thirds between his daughters. But first he expects each daughter to tell him, in the presence of the whole court, how much she loves him. Goneril and Regan do so in hypocritically flowery terms, but when Cordelia's turn comes, she cannot bring herself to compete with her grasping sisters in flattering the old King. Cordelia was Lear's favorite daughter, and he intended spending his remaining years with her. However, her refusal to flatter him so infuriates the stubborn old man that he disinherits her and divides his realm between Goneril and Regan and their husbands, the weak, hen-pecked Duke of Albany and the cruel, power-hungry Duke of Cornwall. Cordelia is given in marriage to the King of France and banished to his country. At this point a middle-aged, bluntly honest and devoted courtier, Kent, objects to Lear's high-handed treatment of Cordelia. He, too, is banished, on pain of death, for intervening on behalf of the wronged daughter. Lear announces that he will now spend alternate months at the houses of Goneril and Regan, and the two vicious sisters plot how to handle the old man and diminish his power in the kingdom.

Now the subplot enters the play. It concerns the superstitious old Earl of Gloucester and his two sons, good-natured, naive Edgar and his cruel, witty, coldly calculating illegitimate brother, Edmund. Edmund sets in motion a plot to disinherit Edgar by telling Gloucester that Edgar is plotting against the father's life. He does so by forging a letter supposedly from Edgar, and the gullible Gloucester believes Edmund's story and promises him the inheritance. Edgar, on Edmund's advice, goes into hiding. He disguises himself as a mad beggar, Tom of Bedlam.

Lear's stay at Goneril's castle is made unhappy by Goneril's insisting that he get rid of his retinue of one hundred knights. She claims that they are ill-behaved, and, backed up by her faithful servant, Oswald, she succeeds in making Lear miserable. One comfort to Lear is that Kent returns, disguised, from his banishment and serves him faithfully again. Another friend, Lear's court jester, or Fool, tries to cheer the King up with his quips and riddles. At the same time, the Fool impresses on Lear the mistake he has made in dividing his kingdom. When Goneril appears, Lear is so incensed by her constant nagging about his retainers that he curses her and storms out of the castle to seek shelter with Regan. Both Lear and Goneril send messages to inform Regan of his approach.

Regan and her husband, Cornwall, have gone to Gloucester's castle on a visit. When Kent, who has brought Lear's note there, meets Oswald, Goneril's servant, Kent beats him for his former insolence to Lear. Cornwall and Regan punish Kent by putting him in the stocks. Gloucester, though he disapproves of what is going on in his own home, can do nothing to stop the fierce pair. When Lear approaches the castle, he is shocked to see his personal messenger in the stocks. He questions Regan about it, but she is obviously on her sister's side and tells Lear to return to Goneril until his month with her is up. Then Goneril arrives, and the two sisters argue with Lear about his retainers, while he curses them both. Lear leaves his ungrateful daughters and rushes out into a storm. In a crude shelter he meets the Fool, Kent (who has been released from the stocks), and Edgar, disguised as a mad beggar to escape his father's wrath.

While Lear and his few friends are braving the storm, Cornwall has become furious with Gloucester for befriending the King.

His anger is aided by Edmund's treachery. Edmund tells Cornwall that Gloucester is a traitor to Britain because he has had dealings with the French army, which has landed at Dover to restore Lear to his throne. Gloucester is captured and his eyes are put out by Cornwall, who is in turn killed for his great cruelty by one of his servants. When Gloucester is blinded, he learns the truth—that Edmund has plotted against him and Edgar is innocent. Gloucester decides to make his way to Dover, where Lear, after the storm, has gone to meet with Cordelia and the rescuing French army.

On the way to Dover Gloucester meets Edgar again, but doesn't recognize his son, who has disguised his voice. Gloucester, in despair, wants to leap off the cliffs of Dover. Edgar fools him into thinking he is on the cliffs. Gloucester jumps but only falls a few feet. Edgar tells him he has had a miraculous escape from death; now he ought to treasure life.

Meanwhile Albany's sympathies have shifted from his wife to Lear. He berates Goneril for her cruelty to her father. But Goneril, in love with Edmund, despises her husband for being weak. She is afraid that because Regan is now a widow, Edmund will marry her. Goneril plots to have Albany killed so that she can marry Edmund. Edmund, now that his father is branded a traitor whose life is forfeit, is the new Earl of Gloucester.

Although Lear finally reaches the French camp at Dover, he feels too much ashamed to meet Cordelia again because of the way he has treated her. Cordelia bears no grudge, however, and sends some soldiers to find her father, who has gone completely mad under the stress of his night out in the storm.

The armies of Albany and Cornwall, now led by Edmund, meet to attack the French. Cordelia is reunited with Lear and assures him that she bears no hatred for his disinheriting her.

Then Oswald, on orders from Regan, tries to kill Gloucester. He is prevented by Edgar, who kills Oswald instead. Edgar gets from Oswald a letter addressed to Edmund. He finds Albany in the British camp and hands him the letter, which tells of Goneril's plans to murder him and marry Edmund.

In the battle between the French and English armies, the French lose, and Edmund captures Lear and Cordelia. He orders that they be executed. Meanwhile, however, Goneril and Regan have been arguing over who is to get Edmund.

Albany produces the incriminating letter he got from Edgar. He accuses Goneril of adultery and challenges Edmund to a duel. Edgar enters, disguised, to fight the duel. He mortally wounds his brother and then reveals who he is. On the point of death Edmund tries to save the lives of Lear and Cordelia, but his message is too late. Edmund dies soon after Goneril, who has poisoned Regan and then stabbed herself. The play ends with Lear bearing in the corpse of Cordelia, who is hanged on Edmund's earlier orders. After recognizing his old retainer, Kent, Lear dies of a broken heart, and Edgar is left to rule the kingdom.

KING LEAR
ACT 1

ACT 1: SCENE 1

The play opens in a room in the palace of King Lear, a legendary ruler of Britain in the time before Britain became fully Christianized. Two noblemen, the Earl of Kent and the Earl of Gloucester (pronounced Glos'ter), are chatting about court politics. From this gossip we discover that Lear, who we later learn is about eighty years old, has decided to divide his kingdom and give up his throne before he dies. He intends to divide Britain among his three daughters, who are named Goneril, Regan and Cordelia.

COMMENT

The oldest daughter, Goneril, is married to the Duke of Albany. The middle daughter, Regan, is married to the Duke of Cornwall. British dukes were second in power only to princes. They generally ruled the area which goes by their name. Thus the Duke of Cornwall rules the southwestern part of England known as Cornwall. Dukes are of much higher rank than earls, like Kent and Gloucester. Cordelia is not married when the play opens, but she is being courted by two French noblemen, the Duke of Burgundy, and the King of France, who is, at the time the play opens, at peace with Britain.

Kent expresses surprise to Gloucester that the kingdom is to be evenly divided. He had thought that Lear liked Albany, Goneril's husband, better than he liked Cornwall, Regan's husband.

COMMENT

This shows that Lear had made up his mind about how Britain was to be divided before the action of the play begins. As it will turn out later, Lear should have liked Albany better than Cornwall, because Albany is by far the more decent man of the two.

In the middle of the discussion between Kent and Gloucester, Kent notices that Gloucester has Edmund, the younger of his two sons, with him. Gloucester tells Kent that Edmund is a bastard whom Gloucester begot with a mistress a year after his legitimate son, Edgar, was born. Kent barely recognizes his friend Gloucester's son, because Edmund has been away from court for nine years. Gloucester jokes lewdly about the fun he had the night Edmund was conceived. He tells Kent that although his property will go by law to the older, legitimate Edgar, he loves Edmund no less, and "the whoreson must be acknowledged."

COMMENT

The tone of this conversation is light and often lewd. Kent and Gloucester establish themselves immediately as two men of the world. There is no sense that Kent either approves or disapproves of Gloucester for the adulterous affair in the past which produced Edmund. The remarkable thing is that neither Kent nor Gloucester is in any way embarrassed at talking about Edmund in his presence. Coleridge thought that this conversation about Edmund's bastardy was embarrassing to him. There seems to be no hint of this in the text. Edmund, like his father, is "brazed to it." See his soliloquy in Scene 2, where he seems to celebrate his bastardy.

The worldly, realistic tone changes abruptly when a trumpet flourish announces the entrance of Lear accompanied by his three daughters, his two sons-in-law, and various courtiers, or nobles who serve the king in his palace. Lear reaches for a map of Britain and announces his intention to divide the kingdom so that he can "Unburthen'd crawl toward death." (This is ironic, as the play turns out, because the division of the kingdom increases, rather than decreases, Lear's burdens.)

COMMENT

There is a fairy tale quality in this scene. There are three

daughters, one virtuous, two evil (as in *Cinderella*); the
kingdom is to be divided into three parts, this being the
magic number in myth and fairy tale. Lear makes something of a ritual of his division; notice the pomposity
and long-windedness of Lear's abdication speech. There
is much that is ritualistic about the way in which Lear
goes about dividing the kingdom. The whole structure
of the scene is absolutely symmetrical until Cordelia
upsets the apple cart.

Later, the reader will be able to contrast this scene, with
the rich court, the foreign notables, the many courtiers,
with the scene on the heath in Act III, where Lear has
only a fool and a madman to attend upon him.

Lear announces the way in which he will portion out his lands.
There is a catch to it, although he doesn't think of it as such.
Before Lear gives each daughter her third of the kingdom, she
must tell him how much she loves him. Goneril, the oldest
daughter, is called on first. She has no trouble making a glib,
hypocritical speech. She tells Lear that she loves him "Dearer
than eyesight, space and liberty," and, indeed, "no less than
life" itself. Regan makes a similar speech. But while Lear is
lapping up Goneril's and Regan's praise of him, Cordelia is
nervously wondering what will be left for her to say when her
turn, as youngest daughter, finally comes. (Her problem stems
not from lack of love for Lear, but from her embarrassment at
making flowery, ceremonial speeches.)

Finally Lear turns to Cordelia, and calling her his joy (she has
always been his favorite daughter), asks her what she has to
say about her love for her father. Can her speech draw the
richest third of Britain? But all Cordelia says is "Nothing, my
lord." Lear is thunderstruck at this blow to his ego. "Nothing?"
he asks. "Nothing will come of nothing," he warns her. In
other words, she will be disinherited if she can't find some
praise for her father.

Cordelia, wretched, says she can't make flowery speeches the way her sisters do. She loves her father as much as daughters are supposed to love their fathers: no more, no less. This perfectly reasonable answer infuriates the proud old king. He warns Cordelia that she will lose her dowry: He will disinherit her. He assumes that without a money settlement on her marriage, Cordelia won't be able to get anyone to wed her.

At this point Kent tries to butt in, but Lear warns him not to come "between the dragon and his wrath." Lear banishes Cordelia from his sight and announces that the third of Britain that was supposed to go to her will instead be divided between Goneril and Regan. Lear, accompanied by a retinue of one hundred knights, will spend one month alternately with each daughter.

Again Kent intervenes. He has always loved and faithfully served Lear. Now that Lear is acting rashly and foolishly in disinheriting the daughter who loves him most, Kent feels he must warn the King. Lear furiously orders him out of his sight. Kent replies, "See better, Lear."

COMMENT

Notice Lear's picture of himself. He says, "Come not between the dragon and his wrath," and "The bow is bent and drawn, make from the shaft." He pictures himself as a powerful, invincible ruler.

One of the play's great themes begins to emerge: Note the reference to the difference between mere physical eyesight and real, inward vision.

Driven to a peak of anger by Kent's blunt reply, Lear gives him five days to pack his belongings and leave England. Lear warns him that if on the sixth day Kent is found anywhere in his realm, he will be executed on the spot. Kent answers that as long as Lear is going to be so unreasonable, freedom is outside England and banishment is in England. Kent asks for blessings on Cordelia, warns Goneril and Regan that they had better live up to their words of love, and leaves the court.

COMMENT

In this episode, Kent is shown to be like Cordelia. Both are honest and blunt, but tactless in handling the old king. Kent is unlike most courtiers in the play, who are suave and two-faced. Taking extreme action because he is so little used to being challenged or questioned, Lear makes his second terrible mistake as he misjudges and so sentences Kent; banishment was considered a very severe punishment. And already, in the fairy tale atmosphere of the drama, we intuit that the characters of plain speech will turn out to be sound and loyal, while those who speak with inflated rhetoric will soon prove hollow and false.

Now Gloucester enters with the two suitors for Cordelia's hand, France and Burgundy. Lear announces to Burgundy that if he wants to marry Cordelia, he will have to accept her without a dowry.

When he hears that Cordelia has been disinherited, Burgundy quickly backs out. But the King of France is made of better stuff. He tells Lear he is shocked at this disinheriting of Cordelia, and then announces that he will be glad to marry her even if she comes to him without a penny, for she is "most rich, being poor." In other words he sees that her spirit is rich, and her spirit is what counts. He will bring her back to France with him to live. Lear agrees to the marriage and leaves.

COMMENT

This shows what a shrewd judge of character France is. He was not even present in the room when Cordelia showed herself to be so unlike her hypocritical sisters.

Cordelia now says goodbye to Goneril and Regan. She tells them that she hopes they will be as good as their words to Lear. Goneril's answer is that, being disinherited, Cordelia had better worry now about satisfying her new husband, France, who has taken her without a cent of dowry. (The catty cruelty of Goneril and Regan to Cordelia is very much like the behavior of the older sisters to Cinderella.) Cordelia and France leave. Now that they and Lear are gone, Goneril and Regan discuss the situation cynically and selfishly. Goneril points out to Regan how unreasonable Lear's behavior has been. She is shrewdly worried that everyone in court will notice how peculiar his action was in disinheriting his favorite daughter. Regan answers that their father is probably senile, but, in fact, she says, he has never really known his own mind. Both sisters are worried by Lear's "unruly waywardness" and "unconstant starts," in short, his eccentricity. They talk clear-headedly and unsympathetically about him, as the scene ends.

SUMMARY

This opening scene accomplished a number of important things for the play. We are shown all the major characters in action except Gloucester's legitimate son, Edgar, and the Fool, or court jester. We are witness to the moral slackness of Gloucester who, having fathered a bastard, considers this a matter for joking in the court, instead of something of serious concern. The moral level of the courtiers is not very high. Gloucester will later pay heavily for his lapse of virtue, which took place years before the play begins.

We also see that Lear is a rash and self-centered old man. He stages a whole contest to see who loves him most after he has already decided how to divide his kingdom. It also shows the blunt honesty of Cordelia and Kent, an honesty that borders on the tactless. This is in sharp contrast to Lear's other daughters. In the dialogue between Goneril and Regan at the end of the scene, we see how hypocritical their earlier professions of love to Lear really were. Already we get a sense that they are evil and self-serving women who will stop at nothing to get what they want. On the other hand, Cordelia in her own way is as proud and unbending as her father.

This scene is the longest of the play and from its conflicts comes the action of the entire play; this is unusual in the first scene of any play. The weighty introduction to the action shows Lear's moral blindness as to which of his daughters really loves him and which only pretend to love him. He makes the basic tragic mistake of taking the appearance for the reality. Kent has made the same mistake earlier in the scene, when he comments on how handsome the bastard, Edmund, looks. But ironically, it is Kent who points out to Lear that he should "see better." Much of the play will be concerned with true vision, or insight into character, as opposed to surface vision, which can only see the outward shows of character.

ACT 1: SCENE 2

We are now in Gloucester's castle. Edmund enters carrying a letter which he has forged as part of a plot to get his brother, Edgar, disinherited. Before we find out the contents of the letter, however, Edmund reveals himself to the audience in the first soliloquy of the play.

COMMENT

The soliloquy is a device used by dramatists to let the audience know directly what is going on in the mind of a character. It does not mean that the character is actually talking to himself. Nor does it mean he is addressing the audience directly. The soliloquy is what is in the character's mind, spoken aloud so that the dramatist can get across to us what the character is thinking about. Because no one else is on stage or able to overhear during a soliloquy, the dramatic convention is that the character is telling the absolute truth as he knows it. He doesn't feel he has to conceal anything from himself as he would from another character, if one were present. Shakespeare uses the device most effectively for revelation of character. Modern dramatists rarely use it.

Edmund calls Nature his goddess, saluting her here as the divinity of lust and as one who would crown his illegal efforts to get his brother's land away from him. This is not the Nature to whom Lear later appeals and whom Cordelia, Edgar, and Kent obey, but a naked, selfish individualism, given over to lust and greed. Edmund renounces both religion and the laws of human society, seeing nature in opposition to them. Also, as a bastard, Edmund is a "natural child," meaning he was not born as a result of marriage, a social convention. Edmund is haunted in this soliloquy—and later in the play—by the fact that he is a bastard. He tells himself he is as good a man as his brother, Edgar, and probably a better man. The reason he gives is that more energy is required in an adulterous affair than in normal marriage, so that he was conceived when his father, Gloucester, was really lusty.

"Well then,/ Legitimate Edgar," Edmund sneers, "I must have your land." The letter Edmund has just forged should get it for him. Filled with evil confidence he shouts, "I grow, I prosper;/ Now, gods, stand up for bastards!"

COMMENT
This soliloquy shows that Edmund is ruthless and determined to have his way, and that he has many of the weapons he needs with which to thwart society. He is clever and witty. Ashamed of being a bastard, Edmund is also genuinely scornful of his legitimate, kindly brother, Edgar. Edmund is aware that he is evil by choice, not by necessity. He makes no excuses to himself for his depravity.

Now Gloucester enters, musing distractedly about the speed of the unhappy events in the previous scene. Edmund

cleverly pretends to hide the letter that is in his hand, knowing that doing so will only make his father more curious to
find out what is in it. Edmund refuses to hand the letter over,
saying it isn't fit for his father to read. The more Edmund
refuses, the more Gloucester insists. Finally Edmund gets his
real wish: Gloucester reads the counterfeited letter and is
naturally horrified at its contents.

The letter, supposedly written by Edgar to Edmund, says that
Edgar wishes his father would die soon so that he could
inherit his estate. Edmund adds fuel to the fire now raging in
his father's breast by saying he has often heard Edgar complaining about this point. Gloucester gullibly believes him,
and Edmund's plot is well launched.

COMMENT
This is the first of several important letters in the play.
Many plot points are made by means of letters.

Gloucester, shouting that Edgar is an "Abominable villain,"
asks Edmund where he is. Edmund says he doesn't know, but
will search Edgar out and bring him to Gloucester.

Gloucester blames some recent eclipses of the sun and moon
for the divisions between parents and children and between
friend and friend that he has just seen in the court and now in
his own life. First, Lear has been alienated from his daughter,
Cordelia, and his friend, Kent. Second, Gloucester himself is
now alienated from his son, Edgar. Gloucester says the best
part of his life is over: All that awaits him is "hollowness,
treachery, and all ruinous disorders." When Gloucester leaves,
shaking his head sadly, Edmund, in another soliloquy, makes
fun of his father's gullibility and superstition.

COMMENT
Gloucester is superstitious, but he understands the moral
law and grieves genuinely over the chaos which enters

into human relationships when nature or order is upset by the failure of natural relationships.

Edmund is a skeptic, for he does not believe that the "late eclipses" have any effect on human affairs. Shakespeare would probably have questioned such complete skepticism.

Edgar now enters, and Edmund asks him if he can remember offending their father recently. Edgar says no. Then Edmund, playing a cat-and-mouse game with his naive brother, says that apparently someone has slandered Edgar to his father, because Gloucester is furious with him. He warns Edgar that he had better fly for his life; if Gloucester sees him, he will kill him. Edgar doesn't understand what Edmund is talking about, but being as credulous as his father, he agrees to flee for his safety.

SUMMARY

In this scene, the subplot is set in motion. It follows the fortunes of Gloucester and his sons, Edmund and Edgar, and parallels closely the main plot about Lear and his daughters, Goneril, Regan and Cordelia. Thus two fathers are deceived by their children. Toward the end of the play the two plots will merge.

Edmund reveals himself as a complete schemer and villain. He is like Iago in *Othello,* or Richard III, or the Satan of Milton's *Paradise Lost* because he is a conscious villain. Edmund enjoys being a villain and knows just how wicked he is. He is also witty, like the above-mentioned villains.

We see that Gloucester, like Lear, is too ready to believe what people tell him. Just as Lear is foolish to accept at face value Goneril's and Regan's claims of love, so Gloucester is foolish and blind to accept one son's (Edmund's) slander of another son (Edgar). Gloucester is shown to be religious to the point of superstition, while Edmund is coldly rational and materialistic.

ACT 1: SCENE 3

The scene shifts to the palace of Albany and Goneril. Goneril is complaining to her servant, Oswald, that Lear's retinue of one hundred knights is annoying her and upsetting her household. Lear is apparently spending the first month after abdicating the throne with his eldest daughter and her husband. He has brought with him a band of knights to serve him, and they are not getting along well with the regular household staff. At the moment, Lear is out hunting. Goneril takes this opportunity to tell Oswald that she's had enough of her father and his "riotous" followers. When Lear comes back from his hunting expedition, Goneril wants Oswald to tell him that she's sick and can't speak with him.

Calling Lear an "idle old man," Goneril furthermore tells Oswald that in the future the steward is to ignore any requests her father may make. If the old king objects to this treatment, he can go visit with Regan for a while. Also, she tells Oswald, "let his knights have colder looks among you." In other words, Lear and his retainers are to be totally ignored, if not actually snubbed by Goneril's own servants.

SUMMARY

This is a very short scene—only twenty-seven lines in length. In it, we learn that Goneril is already sick of having her father with her and is planning to make him feel as ill at ease as possible.

An easy way to remember which evil daughter is married to which duke, and which pair Lear visits first, is to remember them alphabetically, as follows: Goneril's name begins with a G, which comes before the R of Regan's name in the alphabet. Goneril is married to Albany, whose name comes alphabetically before Cornwall, Regan's husband. Lear visits first the pair whose names come first in the alphabet: Goneril and Albany.

ACT 1: SCENE 4

Lear returns from the hunt and finds Kent, disguised, waiting to see him. Lear does not recognize his old friend and retainer, whom he banished from England in Scene 1. He asks Kent what he wants, and Kent replies that all he wants is to serve Lear. Kent says he recognizes "authority" in Lear's face and would like to be a loyal retainer. He tells Lear he is forty-eight years old, much younger than he really is. Lear accepts his services.

COMMENT

In recognizing "authority" in Lear's face, Kent is seeing a good deal more than either of the old king's evil daughters can see. His offer of service does much at this point to bolster Lear's sagging spirit.

One of Lear's knights says that he has noticed "a great abatement of kindness" to the old man lately. Lear agrees that he, too, has perceived "a most faint neglect of late," but blames it on his own jealousy and desire for attention. He cannot believe that he is being purposely neglected by Goneril. Then he adds that he "will look further into" the matter.

COMMENT

This turns out to be very ironic, because Lear does indeed look further into his neglect—much further than he ever thought he would have to, or ever wanted to look when he made the statement. Lear's awareness that he is jealous is the first time in the play that he shows any self-criticism.

Then Lear calls for the Fool, or court jester, to cheer him up. The knight tells him, however, that the Fool has been keeping to himself lately, pining for Cordelia, whom he loved, and who is now in France with her husband. The Fool never really recovers from the blow of Cordelia's banishment; in this, he is like a double for Lear's youngest child. (See the conclusion of the play, in which Lear speaks of his "poor Fool.")

Now Oswald enters. He speaks rudely to Lear, and Kent trips him up and sends him sprawling on the floor for his insolence. This act immediately draws Lear together in a new bond with his old, wronged friend, even though he still does not recognize him. He gives Kent some money as a kind of tip. At this point the Fool enters the room.

COMMENT

The Fool is the most mysterious figure in the play. Essentially he is a court jester, and not "foolish" at all. Sometimes, however, he does seem to be on the verge of madness. He has several functions in the play. He teaches Lear wisdom that the King lacks. He can do so by means of wit because of a court convention, or custom, which allows the Fool to say anything he likes to his monarch, even things which would be treasonous coming from anyone else. He also cheers the old King up. At the same time, though, the Fool is often cruel to Lear in much the same way as Goneril and Regan are, that is, in their insisting on showing him to himself for what he is. Probably this cruelty stems from the Fool's love for the banished Cordelia.

The Fool comments on the behavior of all the characters he meets in the play. He can do this because he is not involved in any of the intrigues. He also states the themes of the play.

Once the Fool performs these actions he disappears from the play and is never heard from again. The Fool always talks in riddles and puns. It is often extremely difficult to understand exactly what he is saying at any given moment because his mind is very complex, and the language he uses has become obscure by now. Many words have changed meaning or lost their original meaning entirely over the years. He is also fond of singing snatches of archaic nonsense songs.

In this scene the Fool's jests with Lear all come to one thing: Lear, not the Jester, is the real fool. For Lear has upset the natural order of things by putting himself in his daughters' care. He did the opposite of what Nature intends parents to do with their children. For upsetting this balance of Nature, in which children must obey their parents, Lear will suffer. For instance, when Lear asks the Fool if he is calling his master "fool," the Fool answers: "All thy other titles thou hast given away; that thou wast born with." Kent recognizes the truth behind this remark, and tells Lear, "This is not altogether Fool, my Lord." (This is like Polonius, saying of Hamlet that if he is mad, there's a method to his madness.)

Now Goneril enters, in a hostile mood. She upbraids her father for what she considers the wild and boisterous behavior of his retainers. Lear cannot believe his own daughter could be so harsh with him. He asks, with tragic irony, "Who is it that can tell me who I am?" In other words, if Goneril is talking to me in this manner, can I possibly be the King and her father? The Fool answers, appropriately enough, "Lear's shadow." Goneril persists in her scolding. She complains that Lear's followers have made her palace into a "tavern or a brothel" by "not-to-be-endured riots." This is the final touch. Calling his daughter "Degenerate bastard," Lear orders that his horse be saddled. He will leave the house before his month is up and stay with Regan.

COMMENT

Lear's calling Goneril a bastard, although technically she is his legitimate daughter, links his problem with Gloucester's problem in the subplot.

Albany enters and tries to calm down the enraged king, but succeeds only in making Lear even angrier. Lear shouts at Goneril that she is lying about his knights; they are "of choice and rarest parts." He begins to regret his impatience with Cordelia for a relatively small fault. Beating at his head with his fists, Lear cries, "Beat at this gate, that let thy folly in, / And thy dear judgment out!" Then in tones like those of an Old Testament prophet, he denounces his daughter, at first praying that she be childless. But then he changes his mind and asks Nature to make her bear a child, so "that she may feel / How sharper than a serpent's tooth it is / To have a thankless child!"

COMMENT

This ferocious speech is one of the most magnificent in the play, but Goneril is totally unmoved by it. To her, all it means is that her father is senile. Albany, however, is beginning to sympathize with his father-in-law, and he wonders whether the woman he married may not really be the monster her father claims her to be.

Lear rushes out of the room after making his great speech. While he is out, he evidently learns that Goneril intends for him to dismiss fifty of his knights—half his retinue—for he returns in an even greater rage.

This time he even weeps, although in the speech just before he had begged Nature to make Goneril weep with a parent's sorrow. Instead, against his will, the tears start rolling down his cheeks. Goneril, still unmoved, stands coldly by while Lear threatens that he will get Regan to right the wrong that has been done to him. He keeps saying "I have another daughter" who will be kind to him.

COMMENT

This is ironic because indeed Lear does have another daughter who will be kind to him: Cordelia. But while the audience knows the truth, Lear means Regan when he says it. If anything, Regan will be crueler to him than Goneril. Thus he persists in his misunderstanding of his daughters. The irony consists of the audience knowing something that a character on stage does not.

After Lear storms off, accompanied by Kent and some retainers, Goneril sends Oswald with a letter to her sister, Regan, informing her of the day's events, and warning her of the temper she will find her father in when he arrives at her house.

SUMMARY

This is one of the most important scenes in the play: It shows just how bitter the conflict will be between Lear and his evil daughters. This conflict was hinted at toward the end of Scene 1, when Goneril and Regan cold-bloodedly discussed their father. Again, in Scene 3, when Goneril instructs Oswald to ignore Lear, we get some hint of the conflict. But now it really erupts, and Goneril abuses Lear in no uncertain terms.

At the same time that Lear begins to reap the fruits of his folly in giving his kingdom to Goneril and Regan, he begins to gather around him three important friends. They are the Fool, Kent, and Albany. The Fool has been estranged from Lear ever since the banishment of Cordelia, whom he loved. Now he will try to comfort the King in his anguish and lead him to a true vision of life. In his loyalty to Lear, Kent has refused to accept the banishment meted out to him in Scene 1. Risking his life by remaining in England against Lear's orders, he disguises himself and rejoins Lear. He demonstrates his old loyalty again in this new disguise by tripping up Oswald, Goneril's insolent servant, when Oswald speaks curtly to Lear. Albany changes his loyalties; when he married Goneril he was in love with her. In this scene, however, he begins to get some inkling of what a monster Goneril is. Although he is generally ineffective, Albany eventually does come over to the side of the good people in the play.

The tension reaches its highest pitch so far in the play. This is accomplished by the magnificent poetry of Lear's speeches to

Goneril. The speeches are filled with the angry denunciations and moral fervor of the Old Testament prophets, whom Lear physically resembles with his snowy white beard and heroic stature.

As relief from Lear's speeches we get the jokes, puns and songs of the Fool. Often they are obscure, or lewd, or both. But always they are filled with wisdom about the true order of things. Although the Fool is sarcastic to Lear, it is for the King's own good, and Lear recognizes the friendly intention behind the Fool's caustic jests.

ACT 1: SCENE 5

In this brief scene, Lear asks Kent to deliver a letter explaining to Regan what has just happened at Goneril's house. The letter also says that Lear will be arriving to visit Regan soon. Lear very fair-mindedly tells Kent not to add any details about Lear's miserable reception at Goneril's house to whatever is already in the letter. He warns Kent that if he doesn't hurry, the letter will get to Regan only after Lear arrives.

Kent rushes off with the letter, and the Fool continues his riddles and jokes. Typically, he asks Lear if he knows why a snail has a shell. The answer is that a snail has a shell to keep his head safe, and not to give it to his daughters. Lear is distracted with grief, mixed with a tinge of self-pity. He says of himself, "So kind a father!" The Fool says that if Lear were his fool, he would have him beaten for being old before he was wise. In the midst of this joking, Lear prays tragically: "O! let me not be mad, not mad, sweet heaven."

COMMENT

This is Lear's first inkling that his misery may drive him insane, and there is nothing he can do about it. The fact that Lear is aware of his growing madness makes it all the more tragic.

Characteristic of Shakespeare's love for mixing the tragic with the comic, after this solemn prayer, the scene ends with the Fool making a lewd joke.

SUMMARY

In this short scene, Kent again shows his loyalty by promising to deliver Lear's letter to Regan. Lear shows how deeply he has been hurt in the preceding scene by Goneril. Lear's sending the letter to Regan shows that he expects a kindlier reception from his second daughter. Lear's fear of madness is established. The Fool continues his treatment by wit of what he considers Lear's folly in giving everything to his daughters.

KING LEAR
ACT 2

ACT 2: SCENE 1

We are now in Gloucester's castle. Edmund meets the court-ier, Curan. Curan tells him that Cornwall and Regan will be visiting Gloucester tonight. Curan adds that Cornwall and his brother-in-law, Albany, are feuding, and open war between them is likely to break out.

COMMENT

There is no rational explanation for this feud, except that Goneril and Regan are vicious not only to Lear and Cordelia, but to each other as well. They are involving their husbands in a greedy fight over who is to get more land. The point is that evil is self-defeating because evil people don't know when to stop. They attack each other as well as attacking the innocent, ultimately destroying themselves.

Now Edgar appears. Edmund warns him that Cornwall and Regan are due to arrive at any moment, and rumor has it that Edgar has spoken against them. Gullible as ever, Edgar doesn't understand how this rumor could have gotten started. He still doesn't realize that Edmund is plotting against him. Edmund hears Gloucester approaching and tricks Edgar into drawing his sword and entering a mock duel. Then he tells Edgar to leave and scratches his own arm with his sword. Now, when Gloucester appears, Edmund complains to him that he just got the wound from Edgar. He thus further angers Gloucester against his one good son, Edgar. Gloucester says that Edgar may have escaped just now, but swears he will be caught and punished.

At this point, Cornwall and Regan arrive at Gloucester's castle. Gloucester appeals to them for sympathy, crying that his "old heart is crack'd" about his son's "treason."

COMMENT

This line identifies Gloucester with Lear, whose old heart is also cracked because of his children's behavior. Thus the Lear plot and the Gloucester subplot begin to merge.

Edmund has joined with Regan and Cornwall. He uses every means to frighten Edgar and make him flee. Also, he turns his father still more against Edgar by reporting that he was "mumbling of wicked charms" — which would especially alarm the superstitious Gloucester. Gloucester actually believes that Edgar wanted to kill him and is ready to catch and "dispatch" him.

Regan asks Gloucester if Edgar has been keeping company with her father's "riotous knights." Gloucester says he doesn't know, but Edmund quickly butts in and says yes, "he was of that consort." (This seals Edgar's doom as far as Regan and Cornwall are concerned.) Cornwall compliments Edmund on his devotion as a son in uncovering Edgar's "plot" against his father. Edmund answers smugly and hypocritically, "It was my duty." Neither Regan nor Cornwall show much sympathy for Gloucester's misery as a father, although Regan, calling Gloucester her "good old friend," tells him not to worry. She and her husband will take care of his treacherous son, Edgar.

SUMMARY

This scene establishes that Edmund is determined to continue the plot against Edgar. It also shows that Regan and Cornwall are well mated, for each is ferociously evil. Evil has gained ascendancy: Regan, Cornwall and Edmund have power over the gullible, easily fooled Edgar and Gloucester.

The scene also foreshadows that Regan's reception of Lear will be no kinder than Goneril's was.

ACT 2: SCENE 2

This scene takes place before dawn, in front of Gloucester's castle. The two servants, Lear's Kent and Goneril's Oswald, enter separately, each carrying a letter for Regan. Oswald, pretending not to recognize Kent as the man who tripped him for his insolence to Lear in Act I, suavely asks him where he may leave his horse. But Kent, who can't stand Goneril's hypocritical servant, replies with a torrent of abuse, calling Oswald, among other names, "A knave, a rascal . . . a lily-livered, action-taking whoreson" and a "beggar, coward, pandar, and the son and heir of a mongrel bitch." Kent demands that Oswald draw his sword and fight like a man. When Oswald refuses, Kent starts beating him. Oswald's cries of "murder, murder!" bring Edmund, rapier drawn, to the scene. Edmund asks what the matter is, and Kent offers to teach him a lesson in swordsmanship, too.

By now the whole castle is aroused by the commotion. Cornwall, Regan and Gloucester come out to learn what the matter is. Cornwall asks Kent why he is so furious, and he answers that he is angry that "such a slave as this (Oswald) should wear a sword, / Who wears no honesty." Cornwall's answer is that Kent is the kind of insolent boor who disguises his bad manners as blunt honesty. He calls for the stocks, a device which locks the prisoner's feet so that he cannot move, and makes him an object of mockery to all who see him. He says that Kent will be locked in the stocks until noon, but Regan, typically even more vicious than her husband, changes this order to night. Kent protests that he doesn't mind for himself, but that it is an insult to the King to put his servant in the stocks, which are usually reserved for petty criminals and offenders. Gloucester also begs Cornwall not to punish Kent this way, but to no avail. Kent resignedly whistles himself to sleep in the stocks, bidding "Fortune, good night; / Smile once more; turn thy wheel!"

SUMMARY

This scene doesn't establish many new points or advance the

action of the plot very far, but it does stress some aspects of certain characters in the play, notably Kent's rough, blunt, fierce loyalty to Lear. Kent shows himself unwilling and unable to indulge in the usual court hypocrisy. He says what he means with no flourishes, and no desire to spare anyone's feelings.

Oswald is Kent's counterpart in the Goneril-Albany household. While he is loyal to Goneril, as Kent is to Lear, he is sneaky and cowardly, for he calls for help when Kent challenges him to a duel.

Regan is shown as even crueler than Cornwall. When he wants to put Kent in the stocks only until noon, she insists that the messenger be kept there until night.

Gloucester wants to help Kent, but he is too weak to go against the orders of Cornwall and Regan, even though it is in his own house that they are giving their orders. Placing Kent in the stocks is not only an insult to him, but, more important, an insult to Lear, his master. Cornwall and Regan, hence, are willing to go to any lengths to insult the King.

ACT 2: SCENE 3

This very brief scene (only twenty-one lines long) consists of a soliloquy by Edgar. He is alone in a wood. He reveals that he knows he is being pursued and decides to adopt a disguise. He will pretend to be a harmless idiot beggar, named Tom Turleygood, or Tom of Bedlam.

COMMENT

Bedlam was an insane asylum. The name is an English corruption of Bethlehem. It is ironic that a hospital named after Christ's birthplace should have been filled with miserable, cruelly treated lunatics. A favorite diversion of Londoners used to be to go to Bedlam and make fun of the inmates, sneering at their peculiar behavior.

Bedlam was so crowded that almost any harmless lunatic who preferred to beg alms outside was permitted to do so. The idiot or crippled beggar was a common figure in Shakespeare's day because after Henry VIII closed the monasteries, there was no place for these poor people to seek alms but on the open road. Thus Edgar's choice of a disguise is a reasonable one.

SUMMARY

This scene shows Edgar for the first time taking some action to save himself from his brother's plot. His idea of disguising himself as a mad beggar is that nobody will take a lunatic seriously enough to be suspicious of him. In disguise, he can bide his time until the slander against him has been straightened out. His decision is roughly like Hamlet's decision to act insane in order to avoid the suspicions of his uncle, Claudius. Edgar's disguise as a lunatic has two parallels so far in the play: He is now in disguise, as Kent is, and is pretending to be mad, as Lear is actually going mad.

ACT 2: SCENE 4

We are in front of Gloucester's castle again. Lear, accompanied by the Fool and an unnamed Gentleman, comes upon Kent in the stocks. At first Lear assumes that Kent is just playing a joke by sitting there. When Kent assures him that he was placed in the stocks by Cornwall and Regan, Lear can't believe what he hears. He is sure that they wouldn't dare treat his own servant in this shameful manner.

Kent, however, tells Lear about his encounter with Oswald, and how Goneril's messenger got a much more welcome reception than he did. Lear, in his anguish on hearing this, cries out, "Hysterica passio! down, thou climbing sorrow!" (Hysterica passio is a disease marked by suffocation or choking.) Lear goes into the castle to find out what has happened, leaving the Fool and the Gentleman to comfort Kent in the stocks. Lear soon comes out of the castle again, amazed that Regan and Cornwall have left word they do not wish to be disturbed. They've said they are tired from their journey to Gloucester's castle and aren't feeling well. At first, Lear is angry, but then is willing to accept the excuse. Still, he is furious that Kent is in the stocks and wants some explanation.

Finally, Gloucester emerges from the castle with Cornwall and Regan. A servant sets Kent free. Lear immediately begins un-burdening himself to Regan. He tells her that Goneril "hath tied / Sharp-tooth'd unkindness, like a vulture here," pointing to his heart. Regan's answer is that Lear should be patient; she can't believe her sister would "scant her duty" to him. She tells her father that he is old and should be more discreet. He should return to Goneril and let her take care of him. Lear again can't believe what he hears. Should he return and ask Goneril's forgiveness? Should he kneel before her and say "Dear daughter, I confess that I am old; / Age is unnecessary: on my knees I beg / That you'll vouchsafe me raiment, bed, and food"? Never!

He begins to curse Goneril, and Regan rightly says that some-day he will curse her too, "when the rash mood is on." Lear says he never would, because Regan is kind where Goneril is cruel. He is about to ask her again why Kent was put in the stocks when he is interrupted by a trumpet announcing the arrival of Goneril. When she enters, Lear asks her if she is not ashamed to look upon his old white beard. But Regan takes her sister's hand, and Lear feels completely betrayed. He gets Cornwall to admit that he was responsible for putting Kent in the stocks. Regan pleads with her father to dismiss half his retinue and return to Goneril. Lear cries out that rather than do that he would live out in the open air, or even beg France for a pension.

COMMENT

As usual, Lear doesn't realize how true are the words he speaks. Before the play ends, he will do both: live in the outdoors, in a storm, without a roof to his head, and receive mercy from France and Cordelia.

Lear tells Goneril that he will stay with Regan and keep his one hundred knights. But now Regan tells him he can't. She isn't prepared to receive him yet, as he wasn't supposed to come to her until the end of the month. Again she urges him to return to Goneril. She asks him why he needs even fifty knights. If he stays with her, he'll have to do with twenty-five. Lear answers tragically, "I gave you all." Regan cruelly counters that he certainly took his time about it. She and Goneril keep arguing with him and finally doubt that he needs even one attendant, and Lear cries, "O! reason not the need."

COMMENT

In a purely logical sense, the sisters' argument is sensible. They have sufficient servants to take care of Lear's needs. What they don't realize, or ignore, is that he is arguing for retaining his knights as a matter of principle. Also, he still wants to keep some of the grandeur he had as King, even after giving up his kingdom. This desire is part of his folly, but it is more understandable than his folly in banishing Cordelia. Lear is arguing for distributive justice. He will distribute superfluity to beggars in the storm scene. The sisters' argument is that retributive justice—what would legally be sufficient—is enough.

Lear cries to the heavens for patience: "You see me here, you Gods, a poor old man, / As full of grief as age; wretched in both!" He vows that he will not weep; instead he'll take revenge on both daughters.

COMMENT

He threatens them with revenge in such a broken and incoherent way that we can see it is a hollow threat.

For the first time, from a distance, we hear the storm which will unleash all its fury on Lear in the next act. Crying again to the Fool that he will "go mad," Lear leaves, followed by Gloucester, Kent and the Fool.

Cornwall, hearing the storm, asks Regan and Goneril to come back into the castle with him. Regan says the castle is too small to house Lear and all his retainers. She will receive him gladly, "but not one follower." Goneril agrees that he has only himself to blame if he is left outdoors in the storm. Gloucester returns and tells the sisters that their father is in a towering rage. Regan coolly answers that this will teach him a lesson: "He is attended with a desperate train" who would abuse her hospitality. Regan orders the doors of the castle to be shut as the storm finally breaks, and the act ends.

SUMMARY

This is a crucial scene in the play for the following reasons: Both daughters behave their worst yet to Lear. His sense of betrayal, when Regan backs up Goneril in her demands that he get rid of his retinue, affects him both mentally and physically. It sends him closer to the brink of madness, onto a deserted, desolate heath just as a storm is breaking. (A heath is like a moor: It is a vast area of wasteland, with only low, scrubby vegetation growing on it.) Heaths figure prominently in *Macbeth, Wuthering Heights,* and *The Return of the Native,* as well as in *King Lear.* They always symbolize man's puniness in the face of a hostile, or at least indifferent, universe.

The scene separates Cornwall from Albany in the extent of their villainy. Albany, when last seen, has begun to sense how evil his wife is. Cornwall, on the other hand, in this scene aids Regan in her nastiness to Lear.

The scene brings the audience's sympathy completely over to Lear's side. Where he might have seemed arbitrary and unjust in earlier scenes, the terrible treatment he receives from both daughters here makes us forget that. It is pitiful to us as Lear becomes a shuttlecock, batted from one daughter to the other. Even his haggling over how many knights he is to keep obviously stems more from a desire to hang on to some remnant of the respect he enjoyed as a King than from mere willful pride. Although one can see how irritating he must have been to have around, the degree of his mental suffering at the hands of his daughters far exceeds any annoyance he may have given them.

There is pathos, then, in the situations of both Lear and Gloucester; the first gives up his rightful place, while the latter's home is taken out of his control. It must be remembered that technically, neither Goneril nor Regan has the right to shut the doors of Gloucester's castle on anybody. But Gloucester, although basically a good man, is too weak to stand up to them.

KING LEAR
ACT 3

ACT 3: SCENE 1

Kent and a Gentleman meet out on the heath. The storm by now has reached full fury. Both men are searching for Lear. The Gentleman tells Kent that he last saw the King "contending with the fretful elements," shouting that the wind could blow the earth into the ocean, as far as he cared, if only the world as it now exists would change or cease to be. The Gentleman also tells Kent that Lear is accompanied only by the Fool, who is trying to keep his spirits up. Kent, in turn, informs the Gentleman of two important developments:

Albany and Cornwall are vying for power and are bringing England to the brink of civil war; and France, hearing of the mistreatment of his father-in-law, has launched an invasion of England.

COMMENT

The hint of the invasion of England shows that though all has gone well up to now with Regan and Goneril, retribution in the form of an invasion from France may be at hand. It is often noted as an inconsistency that the King of France could not have heard of the sisters' treatment of Lear. On stage this would not be noticed.

Kent tells the Gentleman to make his way to Dover, where he will find the invading army. Giving him a ring which will identify him to Cordelia, he tells the Gentleman to inform her of recent developments.

SUMMARY

In this brief scene the plot is advanced in the following ways: We realize anew that the evil sisters are also greedy. They are egging their husbands on to fight each other for more land.

We also are given reason to hope that all is not lost for Lear: Cordelia and her husband are planning an invasion to set him back on the throne and banish the evil sisters and their husbands. This was a delicate matter for Shakespeare because his audience would naturally react strongly against any invasion of England by France. He shows in this scene, however, that the King of France has no interest in capturing and ruling England. He merely wants to make Cordelia happy by rescuing her father from the clutches of Goneril and Regan.

The scene also functions as a quiet interlude between two scenes of immense emotional force. Plot is more important in it than passion.

ACT 3: SCENE 2

On another part of the heath, we find Lear raging against the storm. He defies the winds to crack their cheeks with blowing and calls out for cataracts to drown the earth and for thunderbolts to singe his white head. In this great speech, interrupted only briefly by some sardonic remarks by the Fool, Lear says that Nature, even at her most violent, is not so cruel as his daughters. The elements, indeed, are merely "servile ministers," because they combine with Lear's daughters to make him wretched. If the storm could accomplish just one thing— destroy the mould of Nature from which "ungrateful man" comes—it would be justified in Lear's eyes, even though he suffers in the process.

COMMENT

The great storm could be taken as a metaphor, or symbol, of the storm which rages in Lear's mind. Because he is a king, a great man on whom the good of his people depends, his stormy moods are reflected in Nature. The storm also represents the upsetting of the order of Nature which Lear caused by making his daughters his masters. This storm scene is the first of several key scenes in the play which are very difficult to stage believably. The power of Lear's language makes any physical storm, produced by wind machines and other sound and lighting effects, seem puny by comparison.

As Lear raves, the Fool keeps trying to comfort him with jests and snatches of song. Then Kent enters. He is shocked to see his sovereign out in this weather, bareheaded and accompanied only by his Fool. Even "things that love night / Love not such nights as these," Kent says. Since he reached manhood, he has not seen "Such sheets of fire, such bursts of horrid thunder, / Such groans of roaring wind and rain."

To Lear, however, the storm represents a kind of wild justice taken by the "great Gods" against sinful man. Nevertheless, he himself, he feels, is a man "more sinned against than sinning." (Ironically, the real sinners, of course, are comfortably indoors.) Kent tries to persuade Lear to take temporary shelter in a hovel or hut nearby, while he attempts to force Regan and Cornwall to open their gates to Lear. The King, in his misery, feels his "wits begin to turn"—in other words, he is going mad. However, he agrees to find temporary shelter, even in a peasant hovel, because necessity "can make vile things precious." He goes off with the Fool, who sings an adaptation of the popular Elizabethan song. "The rain it raineth every day," which Feste also sings in *Twelfth Night.*

COMMENT
By accepting the proposal that he seek shelter in a lowly hut, Lear shows that he is beginning to learn to divest himself of worldly pomp and possessions. At the beginning of the play, in all his courtly splendor, he would never have dreamt of taking shelter in a peasant's hut.

SUMMARY
The value of this scene is essentially poetic. Unlike the preceding scene, in which important plot points are given, here nothing "happens," except in Lear's tortured mind.

Although Lear is not yet totally mad, his mind is failing. He and Kent and the Fool talk at cross-purposes. Among the points stressed in this scene are man's puniness and isolation in the face of an overwhelming universe which is indifferent to what goes on in it; the fact that, cruel as Nature can be, it is not nearly so cruel as human beings. We also get proof of the stubborn, practical loyalty of Kent who will not abandon the king in his misery. Too, the scene shows the loyalty of the Fool. Although he continues his jests at Lear's expense and is himself terrified of the storm, he sticks by his master.

The great poetic effect of the storm itself works in several ways. It is a metaphor for the turbulent emotions within Lear and a demonstration of the chaos produced in Nature when any part of it is upset or overturned. This happened when Lear attempted to buy the love of his daughters, disowned Cordelia, and ultimately allowed his children to rule him instead of his ruling them. This upsetting of the balance of nature was discussed in Act 1, Scene 2, by Gloucester, when he noted that the "late eclipses in the sun and moon portend no good to us."

The difficulty of staging this storm scene has led to one of the most famous critical comments about *King Lear*. This is the statement by Charles Lamb, the nineteenth-century English essayist, that Lear is more effective when read to oneself in the study than when seen on the stage, because "the Lear of Shakespeare cannot be acted. The contemptible machinery by which they mimic the storm which he goes out in, is not more inadequate to represent the horrors of the real elements, than any actor can be to represent Lear. . . ." Even today, with more ingenious stage machinery, the actual storm is never as effective as Lear's words about it. In Shakespeare's day the scene was performed in broad daylight on an open stage, with no attempt at sound or lighting effects.

ACT 3: SCENE 3

We move, in this scene, from the heath to a room in Gloucester's castle. Gloucester is bemoaning to Edmund the fact that he was forced by Regan and Cornwall to lock the doors of his own house against Lear. In addition, they warned Gloucester "on pain of perpetual displeasure neither to speak of (Lear), entreat for him, or any way sustain him." Edmund hypocritically calls this behavior "most savage and unnatural."

Then Gloucester makes a fatal mistake. He tells his son the news that there is a rift between Albany and Cornwall, and, more important, that he has a letter announcing the invasion of England by France to "revenge" the "injuries the King now bears." Realizing how dangerous it is to have such a treasonable letter in his possession, Gloucester has locked it up for safekeeping. He then tells Edmund that he is going out to search for Lear, even if he is killed for doing so. If Regan and Cornwall should ask Edmund where Gloucester is, Edmund is to tell them that he is ill and has gone to bed.

No sooner does Gloucester leave than Edmund decides to retail the information he has received to Cornwall. Gloucester will be a double traitor in Cornwall's eyes, because Cornwall has forbidden him to help the King and because Gloucester has a treasonous letter in his possession telling about the invasion from France.

Edmund soliloquizes after his father leaves that "the younger rises when the old doth fall." In other words, he is perfectly cold-blooded about betraying his father. If Gloucester is executed for "treason," Edmund will inherit his property.

SUMMARY

In this short scene we are shown a number of things about Gloucester and Edmund. We see Gloucester's essential soft-heartedness: He is miserable about allowing Lear to be locked

out of his house. Now he will try to make it up to Lear by
going in search of him. However, he and Lear will be undone
by Gloucester's continued naivete. He tells his son secrets
which could get him in trouble with Cornwall: that he is
going out to search for Lear against Cornwall's orders; that he
has heard of a civil war brewing between Albany and Cornwall;
that he has in his possession a letter telling of the invasion
from France to right the wrong done to Lear. Although
Gloucester is sufficiently prudent to keep the letter from France
hidden under lock and key, he is extremely foolhardy in
letting Edmund know that he has it.

Gloucester's weakness is shown in two ways: He has allowed
his own castle to be taken over by Cornwall, and he lets
Cornwall dictate to him what his behavior ought to be to Lear.

Another aspect of Edmund's villainy appears. He is now plotting not only to get his brother disinherited by slandering him
to Gloucester, but also to get his father into grave trouble by
telling Cornwall he is a traitor. His justification for so callous
an act is that Nature—his "goddess," we remember—dictates
that the old must fall while the young rise in fortune. By
possibly getting his father executed, he is merely speeding up
the inevitable processes of Nature.

ACT 3: SCENE 4

We are now in front of the hovel to which Kent has led Lear
and the Fool. The storm is still raging. Kent tries to persuade
Lear to enter, saying "the tyranny of the open night's too rough
/ For nature to endure." But Lear answers that it would break
his heart to take shelter from the storm because then he would
be free to think about his ungrateful daughters. He prefers to
endure the storm, he says, because at least that keeps his
mind off Goneril and Regan. "Pour on," he defies the storm,
"I will endure." But then his resolution begins to weaken, and
he cries, "O Regan, Goneril! / Your old kind father, whose frank
heart gave all. . . ." He then breaks off, realizing that brooding

about how his daughters have wronged him will lead him directly to madness.

COMMENT

There is more than a trace of self-pity in Lear, as his reference to himself as a kind father shows. He has also claimed, we remember, that he is "more sinned against than sinning." This self-pity does not detract from his grandeur or make his situation any less genuinely tragic; it merely makes him more believable as a human being.

Lear tells the Fool to go into the hovel first while he waits outside. He will pray and then sleep. After the Fool enters the shack, Lear voices a magnificent prayer for all the "poor naked wretches," wherever they are, who must "bide the pelting of this pitiless storm." He realizes now, in his own wretchedness, that when he was King, he had taken too little care of his poverty-stricken subjects. Now he has learned true compassion for the physically miserable of the world. "Take physic [medicine], Pomp," he cries, "Expose thyself to feel what wretches feel."

Lear's meditation is abruptly broken by Edgar, who, dressed as the madman, Tom of Bedlam, shouts from within the hut. Apparently he had taken shelter there before Lear arrived. In a minute the Fool comes rushing out shouting that he's seen a ghost inside the hut. Kent takes command of the situation, calling into the hut for whoever it is to come out. Edgar finally emerges, and, pretending to be mad, cries, "Away! the foul fiend follows me."

COMMENT

Edgar's feigned madness takes the form of a religious persecution mania. He is always fretting about "the foul fiend," meaning Satan. And in reality he is being pursued by a genuine, human "foul fiend," his brother Edmund.

Lear's immediate reaction to the spectacle is that Edgar, too, must have given everything he had to his daughters. Otherwise he couldn't have fallen into such a sorry state. Edgar answers Lear's questions about himself with mad gibberish, frequently referring to the fact that "poor Tom's a-cold." Again Lear comments, with tragic irony, "What! has his daughters brought him to this pass?" He cannot imagine that there could be any other reason for going mad than the ingratitude of children. When Kent assures Lear that Edgar has no daughters, Lear refuses to believe him.

The Fool rightly comments that "this cold night will turn us all to fools and madmen." Indeed, a good deal of the eerie atmosphere of the scene is produced by the fact that Edgar is pretending to be mad, Lear is really going mad, and the Fool, speaking as usual in puns, riddles and snatches of songs, often seems to be mad. Only Kent miraculously retains his sturdy sanity. Lear, listening to Edgar's prattle and seeing him in rags, asks, "Is man no more than this? . . . unaccommodated man is no more but such a poor, bare, forked animal as thou art." (By "forked," Lear means two-legged, like a two-pronged fork.) Again he thinks of the puniness of man in a hostile, or at best indifferent universe. The sheep at least has wool to keep it warm, but without clothing man is a miserable, exposed animal. Indeed, as if proving his point, Lear starts tearing off his clothes, to identify himself with all suffering humanity. The Fool prevails on him, though, to keep some clothing on, because it's "a naughty night to swim in."

Now Gloucester, who has been searching for Lear, enters carrying a torch. Edgar pretends to think he is the devil because of the eerie light which surrounds him. Actually, of course, he is afraid his father will recognize him. It is so dark, though, that at first Gloucester does not see who is there. Nor does he ever recognize Edgar, his own son, in the wretched disguise he has assumed. When Edgar treats him to a typical raving monologue, Gloucester sadly asks Lear, "What! hath your Grace no better company?" He explains to Lear that he is disobeying Regan's and Cornwall's orders to keep his doors barred against the King. He has come to bring Lear to "where both fire and food is ready."

Lear, however, ignores Gloucester's offer, even though Kent, too, urges him to accept. Instead, Lear keeps questioning Edgar, as if he were a learned man. Kent notices this and asks Gloucester to repeat his offer because Lear's "wits begin t' unsettle." Gloucester says he can't blame Lear for going mad; his daughters seek his death. Then he thinks of his own situation and says he is almost mad, too, because he has a son, who though Gloucester loved him dearly, sought his life.

COMMENT
Gloucester is referring, of course, to Edmund's slanderous story about Edgar. It is ironic that he repeats it in Edgar's actual presence, not recognizing his own son in disguise. He is unaware of Edgar's innocence and Edmund's guilt. Yet, note his subconscious reaction to his son. There is no reason so strong as Edgar's actual presence for Gloucester to refer to him at this point.

Seeing that he can't get Lear to stir, Gloucester at last persuades him to take shelter inside the hovel, and they all go in as the scene ends.

SUMMARY
In this weird scene, Lear has finally gone completely mad. In his madness, his humanity begins to emerge, as he prays for the poor and wretched of the whole world. When he was King, he was too powerful to bother much about his miserable subjects. Now that he is reduced to their state, he realizes the cruelty of his former pomp and power. He has developed a social conscience. This is symbolized in the play by clothes. In Act I, Scene 1, Lear was magnificently dressed, complete with crown and sceptre. Now, in this scene, he tries to tear off

his few miserable rags. One of the things he is being forced to learn the hard way is that material possessions are worse than useless and must be shucked off if he is to attain any spiritual grace.

Gloucester's essential goodness is brought out by his disobeying the orders of Regan and Cornwall and coming out in the storm to try to protect and comfort Lear.

We see Edgar for the first time since he has decided to adopt the costume of a mad beggar. It is so effective a disguise that even Gloucester, his own father, doesn't recognize him in it. In this scene, not only is Edgar disguised, but, we remember, Kent also had disguised himself because Lear had banished him from England on pain of death, but Kent is determined still to serve him. Thus, evil goes about openly in the characters of Goneril, Regan, Cornwall and Edmund. But the good must go in disguise.

The scene has a weird, surrealistic quality derived from the wild storm and from the various degrees of madness, real and feigned. The real madness of Lear is getting progressively worse, even though he fears insanity more than anything else. His madness has a brooding, compassionate quality to it that makes him a much more decent man than he was in the first scene of the play, when he was in full possession of his faculties. Although he cannot concentrate on what people are saying and has no desire to look after his own physical well-being, the things he himself says are magnificently compassionate, rather than truly mad.

The Fool, for all his wisdom, seems partially mad himself. He always speaks so cryptically and obscurely anyway that he sounds quite deranged in this scene.

As for Edgar, he does a very good job of feigning lunacy.

ACT 3: SCENE 5

We shift back to the "sane" world of a room in Gloucester's castle. Edmund and Cornwall are alone together. Edmund has just told Cornwall that his father, Gloucester, has been plotting treason. The scene opens with Cornwall saying "I will have my revenge ere I depart this house." (Notice that it never strikes Cornwall as poor behavior for a guest to have "revenge" on his host while in the host's own house.)

Edmund hypocritically says that he is afraid that his loyalty to England will bring him the censure of people because it has been at the expense of his natural loyalty as a son. Edmund shows Cornwall the letter telling of the invasion plans from France. (This is the letter Gloucester had foolishly told his son about in Act III, Scene 3.) "O Heavens!" Edmund hypocritically cries, "that this treason were not, or not I the detector!" Cornwall assures Edmund that whether the report of the invasion in the letter is true or false, Gloucester is still guilty of treason for receiving the letter and, as a traitor, has forfeited his earldom. Cornwall makes Edmund the new Earl of Gloucester and tells him to find his father so that Cornwall can arrest him. In an aside, Edmund says that he'll try to catch his father in the act of comforting Lear, which will make Gloucester even more treasonous in the eyes of Cornwall. But aloud to Cornwall all he says is that he will "persever in my course of loyalty, though the conflict be sore between that and my blood." In other words, he will be loyal to Cornwall, even though his blood, or natural filial loyalty, tells him not to be. Cornwall assures him that he will find "a dearer father (than Gloucester) in my love," and the scene ends with each hypocrite giving assurances of loyalty to the other.

SUMMARY

This scene pushes ahead the subplot, preparing us for its climax in Scene 7. It does this by showing Cornwall increasingly involved in evil. So far he has backed up Regan and Goneril in their mistreatment of Lear, barred the doors of

Gloucester's castle against Lear during a storm, and now vowed to arrest Gloucester as a traitor.

Showing Edmund smoothly and coldly snatching the earldom from his father while Gloucester is still alive, in this scene Shakespeare adds still another dupe—Cornwall—to Edmund's list. He has so far persuaded Gloucester that Edgar is plotting against him; persuaded Edgar that since for some mysterious reason Gloucester is angry at him, he had better flee; and now persuaded Cornwall that Gloucester is a traitor to England.

ACT 3: SCENE 6

We are now in a room in a farmhouse near Gloucester's castle. Gloucester and Kent enter. Gloucester tells Kent that he will try to get some food and additional supplies to make the room more comfortable for the King, and off he goes. Now Lear, Edgar and the Fool come in. Edgar is still muttering gibberish and warning everyone to "beware the foul fiend." The Fool asks Lear one of his typical riddles: "Tell me whether a madman be a gentleman or a yeoman (a farmer)." Lear's answer is that a madman is a king. He is getting good at solving the Fool's riddles.

For a moment Lear thinks of taking military revenge on his daughters ("red burning spits / Come hissing in upon 'em"). Then he abandons this idea and decides to try his daughters for their cruelty. This is another and more pathetic way of revenging himself on his daughters. Calling Edgar "most learned justice," and the Fool "sapient (wise) sir," he tells them to be seated, for the trial is about to begin. Kent tries to bring him to his senses, begging him to lie down and rest, but Lear insists on holding his "trial" first. The first to be arraigned is Goneril, about whom Lear says that "she kick'd the poor King her father." Then Lear "tries" Regan. Meanwhile Kent is appalled at Lear's madness, and Edgar is so much moved by the spectacle of the old man trying two daughters who aren't even there that he begins to weep. He fears his tears will be noticed and his disguise discovered. Lear asks tragically in his "anatomizing" of Regan, "Is there any cause in nature that makes these hard hearts?"

Tiring finally of the mock trial, Lear prepares to go to bed, asking Kent to "draw the curtains." (Evidently in his madness he thinks he is back in his own castle, not in a rude farmhouse.) Then he says, "We'll go to supper i' the' morning," because Gloucester has not yet returned with food, and Lear must go without eating that night. The Fool adds, "And I'll go to bed at noon."

COMMENT

These are the last words we hear from the Fool. After this he disappears mysteriously from the play. Some critics have thought these words have a double meaning, namely, that "bed" means "grave" and that the Fool has a premonition of an untimely death.

Now Gloucester finally gets back. He asks Kent where Lear is. Kent answers that he's there in the hut, but asks Gloucester not to trouble him, because "his wits are gone." Gloucester replies that he has overheard a plot to kill the King. He tells Kent to place the sleeping Lear on a stretcher and carry him to Dover, where he will meet Cordelia and France. He warns Kent to hurry. If he wastes even half an hour, Lear's life, as well as Kent's "stand in assured loss." Kent regrets that Lear can't be allowed to rest undisturbed, but he orders the Fool to help him carry the stretcher away. Kent, Gloucester and the Fool all leave, bearing the King and leaving Edgar alone in the hut to soliloquize that because Lear's sufferings are even greater than his own, they help him to bear his own better. (Because Edgar is alone, his soliloquy is spoken in his own voice, not in the disguised voice of Tom of Bedlam.)

SUMMARY

This scene has the following functions: It shows us Lear at his maddest so far in the play. The "trial" he conducts of Goneril and Regan is both a deadly serious and true indictment, and, at the same time, ridiculous because the defendants aren't there, but are represented by farmstools, and the lawyers are either mad or pretending to be mad.

In this scene, we learn that Regan and Cornwall are determined to have Lear killed. If Lear were dead, the expedition of Cordelia and France to restore him, or at least to aid him, would be robbed of its purpose. Lear is in mortal danger, increased now by his inability to care for himself, but so is anyone caught aiding him. This fact prepares us for the horrible blinding of Gloucester in the next scene. Obviously, Regan and Cornwall will stop at nothing to make sure that justice, in the form of France and Cordelia, will not catch up with them. The greater the threat of invasion, the crueler and more reckless they become.

ACT 3: SCENE 7

This is the most terrifying and blood-curdling scene in the play. It opens in a room in Gloucester's castle on the morning after the storm, with Cornwall telling Goneril to deliver a letter to her husband, Albany. The letter, which is the same one Edmund had stolen from Gloucester, informs Albany that the army of France has landed at Dover. Cornwall is obviously anxious to end the feud with his brother-in-law and unite with him against France. Cornwall also orders a servant to find the "traitor," Gloucester. On hearing Gloucester's name, the bloodthirsty Regan cries, "Hang him instantly." Goneril adds, "Pluck out his eyes." But Cornwall tells the vicious sisters to let him handle the matter in his own way. He asks Edmund to accompany Goneril on her trip home because the punishment he is about to mete out to Gloucester is "not fit for your beholding"; in other words, it will be too horrible for the victim's son to witness.

COMMENT

This desire of Cornwall's to observe all the proprieties by not letting Edmund witness his father's punishment is doubly ironic because it is Edmund who is solely responsible for Gloucester's being in peril in the first place. Nothing Cornwall will do to Gloucester can be as cruel as Edmund's betraying him. And if Cornwall is so proper that he doesn't want Edmund to see what he is going to do to Gloucester, why do it in the first place?

Now Oswald enters, and Cornwall asks him where Lear is. Oswald tells him that the King has been spirited away by Gloucester. Followed by some of his loyal knights, he is now headed for safety in Dover, where France and Cordelia are. Saying hasty farewells to Goneril and Edmund, Cornwall orders some servants to capture Gloucester and bring him back to the castle. He reflects to himself that although he can't give Gloucester a fair trial, his power in the land is so great that while men may blame what he is doing, they can do nothing about it.

In a minute the servants re-enter, bringing in Gloucester as a prisoner. Cornwall orders his arms bound, and the servants tie Gloucester into a chair. The old man cannot understand why he is being treated this way. He reminds Cornwall and Regan that they are his guests in his own castle. Regan's reply is to call Gloucester a "filthy traitor" and to pluck his beard in a traditional gesture of contempt. Gloucester protests his innocence and tells Regan that the white hairs she has just plucked from his beard will come to life and accuse her. Cornwall and Regan now question Gloucester viciously about his alleged treachery and demand to know why he has sent Lear to Dover.

Gloucester answers that he has sent the King to safety because he "would not see thy cruel nails / Pluck out his poor old eyes." (Ironically, this is just what is about to happen to

Gloucester himself.) He tells Regan that if wolves had howled at her gate for shelter from the storm the night before, she would have given it to them, yet she turned out her own father. Gloucester takes comfort in the thought that he "shall see / The winged vengeance overtake such children." But Cornwall, ordering his servants to hold fast the chair to which Gloucester has been tied, assures him he will never see anything again, and proceeds with his thumbs to gouge out one of Gloucester's eyes. The bloodthirsty Regan insists that he gouge out the other eye, too. But before Cornwall can do so, one of his servants, unable to stand the spectacle, begs him to cease. He tells Cornwall that he served him since childhood, but the best service he can do him now is to beg him to let Gloucester alone. Cornwall and the servant now draw swords and begin to fight. The servant wounds Cornwall seriously, but before he can finish him off, Regan grabs a sword and stabs the servant in the back, killing him instantly. Then Cornwall, even though he is in mortal pain, cries, "Out, vile jelly!" and gouges out Gloucester's other eye.

In the depths of his agony, Gloucester cries out for Edmund. But with vicious satisfaction Regan informs him that Edmund hates him and that it was Edmund who let them know of his treachery. Suddenly Gloucester perceives the whole plot against him and cries out at his folly. He prays to the gods to forgive him for abusing his one good son and begs them to bring Edgar to prosperity. Regan orders the servants to thrust Gloucester out of his castle, and, since he is now blind, to "let him smell / His way to Dover."

When a servant leaves, leading Gloucester with him, Regan asks her husband how his wound is. Cornwall first orders Gloucester to be turned out of the castle grounds and the servant who revolted against him to be thrown on a dunghill. Then he replies that he is bleeding badly. Regan helps him out of the room. The two remaining servants comment on the viciousness of their lord and lady and vow to help Gloucester.

One of them will find Tom of Bedlam, who will lead Gloucester to Dover, and the other will apply some ointment to his bleeding wounds.

SUMMARY

In this ferociously barbaric scene, several important things happen. Cornwall has obviously become panicky about the news of an invasion from France. He is trying to enlist the aid of Albany in fighting it, although he himself had been on the brink of civil war with Albany. The two sisters are shown to be at least as vicious as Cornwall. Regan is even more insistent than her husband is about taking fierce revenge on Gloucester. Edmund is shown to be quite willing to desert his father now that he has delivered him into the hands of his bitter enemies.

The actual blinding of Gloucester is significant in at least three ways. It underscores the violence and savagery of the time in which the play takes place. It also shows the absolute depths of despotic cruelty of which a tyrant like Cornwall is capable. Most important, as soon as Gloucester is physically blinded he "sees the light" spiritually. That is, when his eyes are put out and he can no longer see the physical world about him, he "sees" inwardly that Edgar is actually his good son and that Edmund is evil. He sees the injustice he has done Edgar in believing Edmund's slanders against him. Recognizing his folly, he understands that he is being punished. Thus, just as Lear begins to gain insight as he goes mad and when, in the storm, he is deprived of all the physical comforts of the world, so here Gloucester, in the moment of his utmost agony, sees truly for the first time. In this way he is very much like another great tragic figure, Oedipus, who is told of his guilt by a blind soothsayer, and only truly believes it when he puts out his own eyes. One difference, however, between the tragedy of Sophocles and that of Shakespeare, is that Shakespeare has the actual blinding take place on stage. In the Greek play, we only see Oedipus after he has blinded himself.

Regan's nasty comment—that now Gloucester can "smell his way to Dover"—has a deeper meaning than she realizes. The moral stink that she and her husband have made in England can indeed be smelled. The country reeks of crime, treachery and betrayal. The nose, therefore, can prove a more accurate guide to its moral geography than the eyes.

For all the human vileness displayed before the audience's shocked eyes in this scene, certain characters display great nobility. These are:

The first servant. After serving Cornwall all his life, he now turns on him and tries to prevent him from gouging out Gloucester's remaining eye. Shakespeare seems to be saying that even the lowest and most passive people in society will assert themselves for good if pushed far enough by evil power. For Cornwall to be mortally wounded by one of his own servants is most ignominious for him because of the rigid class structure of the time. It was almost unheard of for a servant to disobey his master, let alone turn against him.

The second and third servants. Although they have been silent throughout the scene, they vow at the end to do all they can to aid Gloucester.

Lear's retainers. According to Oswald, at least thirty-five of them are loyally trying to help him get to Dover.

These good people, Lear's retainers and Cornwall's servants, maintain the shaky cause of humanity during the darkest part of the play. They help prepare us for the ultimate humanity of Cordelia while she is off stage. In addition, by pitting the servants against Cornwall and Regan, Shakespeare heightens the element of the conflict between good and evil which dominates the play.

KING LEAR
ACT 4

ACT 4: SCENE 1

This scene, one of the most philosophically rich in the play, takes place on a heath near Gloucester's castle, immediately after the barbaric events of the preceding scene. Edgar enters alone, still disguised as Tom of Bedlam. He philosophizes in a soliloquy that since he has reached the lowest ebb in his fortunes, things can only improve for him. Normally a hopeful and active young man, Edgar refuses to despair. Having hit bottom, he feels he can only rise: "the lamentable change is from the best," he says. "The worst returns to laughter."

But Edgar's hopeful philosophy is shattered by the sight of his father, the blinded Gloucester, who enters at this point. Gloucester, whose eyes are still bleeding, is led by a humble old man, who has been a tenant on the Gloucester estate for eighty years. When Edgar sees the pathetic pair, he cries, "World, world, O world! / But that thy strange mutations make us hate thee, / Life would not yield to age." This is an extension of the philosophical position which he had just taken in his soliloquy. Here Edgar feels that it is only the changes in fortune that chance brings to our lives which reconcile us to growing old and dying. These changes make us hate life so bitterly that we do not mind leaving the world when our time has come. Meanwhile Gloucester, who of course cannot see his son and who doesn't recognize his voice, which Edgar has disguised, tries to get rid of his old tenant. He tells the old man that he can no longer comfort him, and to be seen with Gloucester would be dangerous to him. When the old man protests that Gloucester cannot see his way alone, Gloucester bitterly replies, "I have no way, and therefore want no eyes; / I stumbled when I saw."

COMMENT
This supports the point made in the previous scene, in

which the difference between mere physical sight and true inward vision was dramatized by the putting out of Gloucester's eyes followed by his realization of Edmund's guilt and Edgar's innocence. He means that he stumbled in his attitude to his two sons, as well as in his whole philosophy of life. Now that he is blind he sees truly, and what he sees is that he has no place to go but to death. Gloucester has been contemplating suicide ever since Regan's revelation to him that Edmund, whom he had loved and trusted, had hated and betrayed him.

Gloucester pathetically wishes he might live just long enough to "see" his son Edgar, if only with his sense of touch. (The irony is that he is standing right before Edgar, but doesn't know it. Edgar wants to retain his disguise until he is able to set things right again in his family. It is the only chance he has to defeat his unscrupulous brother.)

The sight of his father plunges Edgar into the depths of pessimism. He has just said that his fortune could only improve. Now he realizes that it has taken a turn for the worse, and may get worse still. In fact, he says, "the worst is not / So long as we can say 'This is the worst.'" In other words, as long as we still have the power of mind to say anything like "this is the worst that can happen," our fortunes can still take a plunge. We can still go mad, or die, and above all, we are not yet entirely without hope.

The old man asks Edgar where he is going, and Gloucester asks whether this stranger (Edgar) is a beggar. When the old man tells Gloucester that Edgar is both a madman and a beggar, Gloucester replies that he must still have some shred of sanity left, or he wouldn't be able to beg. He says he saw a man the night before, in the storm, who reminded him of his son, and who reminds him too of this beggar. Gloucester says that the mad beggar he had seen in the storm (who was, of course, Edgar) was so miserable that he "made me think man a worm." Then Gloucester makes one of the most crushing philosophic statements in the play: "As flies to wanton boys, are we to th' Gods; / They kill us for their sport." The point is that man is destroyed not merely because the gods are indifferent to him; he is destroyed because the gods take a cruel, sadistic glee in crushing him, just as boys enjoy tearing a fly to pieces. This is the most pessimistic religious position taken in the play because it states that evil and suffering in the world are not merely the result of passive indifference, or of chance, but are the result of active, positive cruelty on the part of the gods.

Gloucester again asks the old man to leave him. If he likes, Gloucester says, he may rejoin him further along the road to Dover. But first he asks the old man to procure some clothes for the poor Tom of Bedlam. Meanwhile Gloucester will entrust himself to Tom's care. When the old man protests that the beggar is mad, Gloucester bitterly comments that it is typical of the times that "madmen lead the blind." Finally the old man consents to find some clothes for the almost naked, shivering Edgar. Left alone with his father, Edgar resumes the "mad" patter that he used to disguise himself in the hovel during the storm. Gloucester asks him if he knows the way to Dover and, out of pity for Edgar's mad replies, gives him some money. Gloucester, contemplating suicide, asks Edgar to lead him to one of the high cliffs of Dover. Beyond that point he will not need to be led any further. The pathetic pair leave the stage together.

SUMMARY

The importance of this scene is mainly philosophical. The basic positions taken are as follows: Edgar at first says that once we have reached the lowest ebb in our fortunes, we can be comforted by the thought that they can only improve. This is again the medieval "wheel of fortune" idea which Kent referred to when he was placed in the stocks by Cornwall in Act II, Scene 2. The idea is that a man's life occupies a set position on a great wheel. As the wheel turns, his fortunes rise or fall accordingly. If he starts off at the top, he must inevitably fall; if he starts off at the bottom, he will rise before his inevitable fall, because the wheel is constantly turning. The sight of his father, blind and led by an ancient retainer, makes Edgar modify this view. He now feels that it is good that our fortunes are constantly changing—his own apparently always for the worse—because this makes us hate the world so much that we don't mind leaving it. Then, seeing the full horror of his father's position, Edgar realizes that he was foolish to think he had reached the lowest ebb of his fortunes. As long as we can say, "this is the worst," we can still hope for improvement, so that it is not really the worst that can befall us. The worst comes when we can no longer hope, through madness, despair or death.

Gloucester's philosophy is even more bitter than his son's. He states that since he "stumbled when he saw," in relation to his family, he has no need of eyes. Having sight implies that he has a road to travel in life, but Gloucester is tired of life and wants only to die. He is miserable not only at having had his eyes gouged out, but from the guilt he feels at having disinherited Edgar and trusted Edmund. Man is just a puny worm, at the mercy of the elements, as Gloucester realized in the storm the night before. Also, the gods who rule man's fate are not only not benevolent to him, they are not even indifferent or uncaring. Instead they are consciously and actively sadistic: eager, like boys torturing a fly, only to inflict pain.

The world of men, by which Gloucester means mainly the political and social world, consists of the mad leading the blind. Nevertheless, the extreme pessimism of Gloucester's position does not make him cruel or cynical. When he asks the old man to find clothes for Edgar, it is from a compassionate feeling for all suffering humanity. In this he is very much like Lear, who prayed in Act III, Scene 4, for all the "poor naked wretches," wherever they were, who were exposed to the fury of nature. In that scene Lear regretted his former indifference to the suffering of his people. In this scene Gloucester's only care before he tries to commit suicide is to help out the equally wretched Tom of Bedlam. Gloucester's moving concern, in his misery, for the sufferings of Tom is reflected, too, by the old tenant of his estates, who tries to comfort Gloucester. Even though it is dangerous to be seen aiding Gloucester, the old man refuses to desert him. He is one of the simple, humble people, like Lear's loyal retainers and Cornwall's mutinous servants, who are innately decent and good.

The help that Edgar gives to his father parallels the main plot, where Cordelia helps Lear.

ACT 4: SCENE 2
This scene takes place the following day, in front of the Duke of Albany's palace. Goneril and Edmund have just arrived after their trip from Gloucester's castle. Goneril welcomes Edmund to her home but expresses surprise that Albany is not on hand to greet them. She asks Oswald, who enters at this point, where his master is. Oswald tells her that a great change has come over Albany. When Oswald told him that France had landed an army at Dover, Albany merely smiled at the news. When told that Goneril was coming home, Albany had curtly commented, "the worse." In short, Oswald complains, "What most he should dislike seems pleasant to him; / What like, offensive."

Goneril's response to this news is that her "mild husband" is probably too frightened to fight against the French invasion. She scornfully tells Edmund about the "cowish terror" of her husband's spirit, and asks Edmund to return to Gloucester's castle and hasten Cornwall's war preparations. Hinting that she would not take it amiss if Edmund were to murder Albany some day, she gives him a "favor," or souvenir, and a kiss, and speeds him on his way.

COMMENT

Obviously Goneril's latent love for Edmund has blos-
somed during their journey alone from Gloucester's castle
to her home. In Albany's moral scruples about the plot
she has involved him in, she sees only weakness and
effeminacy. The contrast between her dull, sedate
husband, and the virile, unscrupulous Edmund has
begun to grate on Goneril's nerves, and she is about to
add marital infidelity to her other sins.

As soon as Edmund is gone, Albany enters. Goneril sarcasti-
cally comments on his delay in greeting her, sneering, "I have
been worth the whistle." Albany, however, loses no time, in
upbraiding her for her behavior. "O Goneril!" he cries, "You
are not worth the dust which the rude wind / Blows in your
face." He accuses her and Regan of being "Tigers, not daughters" for their behavior to their father. He is amazed that
Cornwall allowed them to lock Lear out in the storm
(obviously he doesn't know Cornwall), and foretells that if
the heavens don't tame such wild offenses, then "Humanity
must perforce prey on itself / Like monsters of the deep."
(This, of course, is precisely what is happening throughout
the play.)

Goneril's only reply to this richly deserved tongue-lashing is
to accuse Albany of being a "milk-liver'd man," in short, a
coward, for not arming against France. The argument heightens in intensity, with Albany finally shouting that if he were
not a man and Goneril were not a woman, he would tear
apart her flesh and bones. Goneril sneers at this statement,
coolly and contemptuously like a great cat, "Marry, your manhood—mew!"

At this point, a messenger enters with the news that Cornwall
has died of the wounds inflicted on him by his servant. It is
the first Albany has heard of the putting out of Gloucester's
eyes. He is torn between horror at that monstrous act and

relief at the swift justice that overtook Cornwall for committing it "This shows you are above, / You justicers," Albany
exults, "that these our nether crimes / So speedily can venge!"
In other words, to him the stabbing of Cornwall by the
servant is a demonstration that the gods are just, and that they
act speedily to punish the criminal, even if, ironically, they do
it through a mere servant. This is one of the more optimistic
statements of belief in the play.

The news of Cornwall's death has a very different effect on
Goneril. To her, it is both good and bad. The good part is that
with Cornwall dead, she may be able to usurp his and her
sister's part of the kingdom. The bad part is that now Regan
as a widow may be able to marry Edmund. To make matters
worse, Goneril herself has just sent Edmund to Regan, thus
allowing them plenty of opportunity to scheme against her,
while she is stuck with her now distasteful husband, Albany.
She must have time to think; hence, she takes a letter the
messenger has brought her from her sister and retires within
the palace with the excuse that she must read and answer it.

Albany asks the messenger where Edmund was all the time
that Gloucester was being tortured. The messenger replies
that Edmund was escorting Goneril home and has since
departed again. Did he know what was being done to his
father, Albany asks? Not only did he know, the messenger
replies, but it was Edmund who betrayed Gloucester in the
first place. Albany swears to "revenge" Gloucester's eyes and
to thank him for the love and loyalty he showed to King Lear.

SUMMARY

Several new plot developments take place in this scene. Goneril
and Edmund arrive at the Duke of Albany's castle, after a trip
which has apparently solidified their adulterous love for each
other. Albany has by now evidently gone over completely to
the "good" side in the play. He refuses to arm against the
French invasion, and he swears to avenge the tortures under-

gone by Lear and Gloucester. He has come to the vision that humanity will prey on itself like sharks unless the evil train of events is stopped. This is the true Shakespearean vision of the power of one crime or sin, left unchecked, to bring moral chaos and anarchy on the world. Albany and Goneril are now quite openly at war with each other; Goneril is frantic at the thought that the death of Cornwall will leave the way open for Edmund and Regan to marry. What she wants is for Edmund to kill Albany and marry her. Then they can take over Regan's portion of the kingdom for themselves. This scene launches the complex and vicious infighting among the three major evil characters left alive: Goneril, Regan and Edmund. Their passionate scheming will eventually lead to their own deaths.

The balance of power against Lear has been diminished by two important characters: Cornwall is dead, and Albany's sympathies are now on Lear's side. Oswald, however, remains in character by being loyal to Goneril and treacherous to Albany. He tells Goneril of her husband's shift of sympathies with smirking satisfaction.

The animal imagery which runs through the play reaches a peak of savagery here. Goneril compares Albany to a cow, and Albany, in turn, compares Goneril and Regan to tigers and to sea monsters. Finally, Goneril actually mews at her husband like a great cat. The significance of the imagery is that when human beings lose their humanity and begin behaving like animals, they turn the normal social world into a beastly jungle, where no code of ethics or morality reigns except vicious self-interest.

ACT 4: SCENE 3

This scene provides necessary relief and contrast from the squabbling between Albany and Goneril in the preceding scene. It consists of a quiet conversation between Kent and a Gentleman in the French camp near Dover. Kent learns from the Gentleman that the King of France has had to return home on urgent business which required his personal attention. He has left behind him in Dover Cordelia and a Marshal of France, one Monsieur La Far, to conduct the campaign in his absence. The Gentleman is the same one who was sent by Kent to Cordelia in Act III, Scene 1, bearing letters telling her of the mistreatment of Lear. Kent now asks him what her reaction was to the news of Lear's suffering. The Gentleman reports that she simultaneously wept with sorrow and smiled with patience, shaking "holy water from her heavenly eyes." Kent, marvelling at the difference between Cordelia and her sisters, muses that "It is the stars, / The stars above us, govern our conditions; / Else one self mate and make could not beget / Such different issues." In other words, man is ruled by an unalterable destiny which he cannot understand. Otherwise how can one explain a Cordelia and a Goneril or Regan being born to the same parents?

Kent then tells the Gentleman that although Lear has arrived in Dover, he refuses to see Cordelia for shame at having given "her dear rights / To his dog-hearted daughters." The Gentleman says that Albany's and Cornwall's armies are on the march, and the scene ends with Kent begging the Gentleman to put up a little longer with his disguise: Kent will reveal himself when the time is ripe.

SUMMARY
This brief scene, in addition to providing emotional relief, contains the following plot points: After successfully landing an invasion army at Dover, the King of France had to return on urgent business, leaving behind him Cordelia and a Marshal in charge of the army. Cordelia has demonstrated her saintly nobility and forgiveness on hearing of the ill treatment her father had received at the hands of Goneril and Regan. Although Lear has arrived safely at Dover, he is too embarrassed to meet Cordelia, fearing she will not forgive him for the wrongs he has done her. Even though Cornwall is dead, his army is still marching with Albany's against the Dover encampment.

ACT 4: SCENE 4

Amid a flourish of drums and flags in the French camp, Cordelia enters, accompanied by a doctor and some soldiers. Apparently some time has elapsed since the last scene. In that time, Cordelia has received a distressing report about her father. Lear has managed to wander away, in his madness, from the attendants who were supposed to guard him. Cordelia tells the doctor that her father was seen, completely mad, singing aloud and dressed with a variety of flowers. She tells a soldier to send out a hundred troops to look for the King and bring him back to the camp. Then she asks the doctor if there is anything he can do to restore Lear's senses to him. Whoever can do that, Cordelia says, can have all her possessions. The doctor replies that the only treatment he can prescribe for Lear is rest, the "foster-nurse of nature." Cordelia again begs the troops to go in search of Lear, lest, in his insanity, he come to some harm.

Now a messenger arrives with the news that the armies of Albany and Cornwall are fast approaching. Cordelia answers that she is prepared for them. She stresses the point that if there is war, it will be to save her father, not because of any "blown ambition" on France's part. With a prayer that she may soon see her father again, the scene ends.

SUMMARY

In this short scene we learn that Lear, no longer capable of taking care of himself, has escaped from his guards. The news brings out Cordelia's deep concern for her father, and shows a new maturity in her love for him. There are other important points made in the scene. Cordelia's statement that the armies of France are in England not for any territorial ambition, but to restore Lear to his rights, is very important because Shakespeare's audience was fiercely patriotic and would have been highly suspicious of Cordelia because she was connected with a foreign invasion of England. Patriotism is the reason for Albany joining his army with Cornwall's, even though he now despises Cornwall, Edmund and their whole plot. Nevertheless Albany feels required, as a loyal Englishman, to help repel any French invasion, however noble its purpose.

There are at least two echoes of incidents in other Shakespeare plays in this scene. They are Lear decking himself with flowers in his madness like the mad Ophelia wearing flowers in her death scene in *Hamlet;* and the doctor's recommendation of rest as the only possible cure for madness like the doctor recommending rest for the sleepwalking Lady Macbeth.

ACT 4: SCENE 5

We are back in Gloucester's castle, where Regan has remained after Cornwall's death. She is questioning Oswald, who has just arrived with Goneril's letter for Edmund. Regan asks Oswald if Albany's troops are on the move, and if Albany is leading them. Oswald snidely tells her that while the army is indeed marching, with Albany at the head, Goneril is "the better soldier" than her husband. Then Regan tries to pry loose from Oswald some information about the letter which was given him in Act IV, Scene 2. Oswald pretends ignorance out of loyalty to his mistress. Regan tells him he can't deliver the letter to Edmund there anyway, because Edmund has gone off to kill Gloucester and to find out how strong the French army is. Letting Gloucester live after blinding him, she tells Oswald, was a great mistake. Wherever he goes in his wretchedness he arouses "all hearts against us." According to her, however, Edmund's motive in killing his father will be "pity of his misery."

Then Regan tries desperately to keep Oswald at the castle, thus making sure that he can't deliver the letter from her sister. She tells him that the roads are dangerous now, with all the troops marching about, but Oswald remains loyal to Goneril and insists on leaving in search of Edmund. Regan then tries to win Oswald over to her side by assuring him that she knows what is going on in the Albany household anyway. "I know your Lady does not love her husband," she tells Oswald. (How much she loved her own husband is shown by her running after Edmund the minute Cornwall is dead.) She assures Oswald that it is "more convenient" for Edmund to marry her, now that she is a widow, than for him to wed the still-married Goneril. Finally, despairing of ever getting Oswald over to her side, Regan tells him he will benefit greatly if he should happen to encounter Gloucester and kill him, and she sends him on his way.

SUMMARY

This brief scene is mainly concerned with the passionate rivalry between Goneril and Regan for the hand of Edmund. Regan remains at Gloucester's castle after her husband's death, probably in order to be with Edmund, who is the new Earl of Gloucester. She is consumed with desire for Edmund, who has temporarily left in order to find and kill Gloucester; the blinded old gentleman has been arousing too much sympathy among the people who see him. He will also spy on the French army at Dover to see how powerful it is.

Goneril, also desperately wanting Edmund, has sent Oswald to find him at Gloucester's castle, not knowing that he has already left. Oswald remains loyal to Goneril, although certainly not to Albany, of whom he speaks in disparaging terms. This steadfast loyalty to his mistress is the one good thing about Oswald, although one wonders what it is in Goneril that can inspire it. Oswald will suffer in the next scene for placing his loyalty in the wrong hands.

Regan still keeps up some pretense to goodness; she tells Oswald that Edmund is out to kill Gloucester, his own father, for reasons of "mercy."

ACT 4: SCENE 6

This is one of the most crucial and difficult scenes in the play. We are in the countryside near Dover where Edgar, disguised as a peasant in the clothing Gloucester's old tenant had found for him in Act IV, Scene 1, is leading his blind father. Gloucester's only thought now is of suicide. He wants Edgar to lead him to the top of one of the steep cliffs of Dover, where he will leap into the sea below. But Edgar has other plans. He will tell his father they have reached the cliff's edge when, in fact, they are on level ground. Then, when his father jumps, and, of course, doesn't die, Edgar will tell him that he has been spared because the gods want him to live. Given Gloucester's superstition, Edgar hopes that this "miracle" will give him the strength to continue existing and to recognize his son.

As father and son progress, though, Gloucester's suspicions are aroused. Edgar tells him that they are climbing a "horrible steep" hill, but Gloucester rightly maintains "the ground is even." Edgar asks him if he can't hear the sea roaring below them, and when Gloucester says he can't, Edgar replies that his sense of hearing must be affected by his loss of sight. Then Edgar paints a most ingenious picture of how tiny everything below them is. The crows seems as small as beetles; the fishermen on the beach look like mice, and so forth. Gloucester finally seems convinced and bids Edgar leave him there, giving him his purse as a reward for leading him this far.

Then Gloucester kneels and prays to the "mighty Gods," renouncing the world and saying he cannot bear to be in it any longer. He throws himself forward and falls, fainting with the thought that he has leapt off a cliff. Edgar rushes up to him, awakens him, and says he has fallen "many fathom down." It is a miracle he is still alive, Edgar says. He should have been broken like an egg. Gloucester is merely disappointed that he hasn't in fact died. Edgar helps him to his feet, saying that the beggar who led him to the edge of the cliff was some fiend so that Gloucester can attribute his life to the fact that the gods wished to preserve him. Gloucester vows to bear his affliction until the end and not try to commit suicide again.

COMMENT

Gloucester's attempted suicide is one of the three most difficult scenes in Lear to stage effectively. (The other two are the storm scene and the blinding of Gloucester.) The problem is that the audience sees that Gloucester is not really leaping off a cliff, but is merely falling on level ground. For this reason it is difficult to keep the scene from becoming unintentionally funny. The illusion is helped, however, by Edgar's ingenious poetic description of the imaginary tiny figures on the beach below. Furthermore, some modern directors see the scene as intentionally comic, in the tradition of mad, pessimistic humor that is now called "theatre of the absurd."

At this point Lear enters, dressed in wild flowers, as Cordelia had described him in Act IV, Scene 4. He has eluded his attendants and is wandering madly about, claiming at one point to be a counterfeiter, at another a recruiting officer, then an expert bowman and a sentry. Beneath all his incoherent babble, however, there is a good deal of sane comment on the state of the world. Edgar and Gloucester are struck with horror at the spectacle of the mad King. Gloucester seems to recognize Lear's voice, and asks, "Is't not the King?" Lear answers magnificently, "Ay, every inch a King." But then he ironically adds, "When I do stare, see how the subject quakes." Again, as in Act III, Scene 6, he holds a kind of mock trial, but this time all nature, not merely his daughters, is arraigned. No one shall be executed for adultery from now on, Lear maintains, because the whole natural world, down to the tiniest wrens and flies, is promiscuous. Besides, Lear says bitterly, "Gloucester's bastard son / Was kinder to his father than my daughters / Got 'tween lawful sheets."

COMMENT

Lear is constantly obsessed with the idea that his daughters cannot be legitimate, because he can't understand how he could have begotten such vicious creatures. Here he turns the idea around and realizes that legitimacy is no guarantee of decency: The bastard Edmund was kinder to his father than Lear's legitimate daughters were to him. Of course, we know what Lear doesn't know, that Edmund is just as vicious as Goneril and Regan.

Then Lear rages against women and sex in general; the "riotous appetite," as he calls it. In sex, he says, is "hell, there's darkness, there is the sulphurous pit." He is totally revolted by the constant sexual maneuverings throughout all nature and holds women especially responsible for them. Gloucester, moved deeply by Lear's words, cries, "O! let me kiss that hand." But Lear replies, "Let me wipe it first; it smells of mortality."

COMMENT

"Mortality" has two meanings here: Death, in that Lear foresees his impending death, with all the attendant stink of corruption, and Life, in the sense of being mortal; being human and alive. Here he means that just being alive involves moral stench and corruption. In this sense, the smell of Lear's hand may be considered one of the ways in which Gloucester can "smell his way to Dover."

Calling Lear a "ruin'd piece of Nature," Gloucester asks if the King recognizes him. Lear says that Gloucester must be blind Cupid, and warns Gloucester that he will never make him love. Lear adds that Gloucester doesn't need eyes to "see how this world goes." The law of the world, Lear explains, is that there is no difference between judge and criminal. It is just a matter of who is in the more powerful position, for we are all guilty. In his disgust with the world, Lear catalogues all the injustices, all the ways in which people in power get away with the same crimes for which they savagely punish the less powerful. Such is the eloquence of his speech that Edgar turns aside and comments, "O! matter and impertinency mix'd; / Reason in madness."

Then Lear tells Gloucester that he really does know him and says he must be patient about dying; we can no more control the time of our death than the time of our birth, and "when we are born," Lear adds, "we cry that we are come / To this great stage of fools." Lear then abruptly thinks of his sons-in-law (he doesn't yet know of Albany's sympathy for him) and cries, "kill, kill, kill, kill, kill, kill!"

At this point Lear's attendants catch up with him and try to reason with him to go to Cordelia. But Lear thinks he is being taken prisoner and tells them that if they treat him well, they will get ransom. Then he mockingly bids them catch him and dashes off, leading the attendants quite a chase. Edgar asks the Gentleman who has come with Lear's attendants how near the armies of Albany and Cornwall are. The Gentleman says that they are very close and are about to engage in battle with the French army.

Suddenly Oswald enters, overjoyed that he has found Gloucester, so that he can kill him and gain the prize Regan promised him. But Edgar steps forward in defense of his father and speaks insultingly to Oswald in broad peasant dialect. Oswald is infuriated that a lowly peasant should interfere with his killing of Gloucester, and he begins to duel with Edgar. But Edgar quickly knocks him down, fatally wounding him. Before Oswald dies, he begs Edgar to deliver his letter to Edmund. But, once Oswald is dead, Edgar of course rips open the letter and discovers in it that Goneril is proposing to Edmund that he kill Albany and then marry her. Suddenly the drums of war are heard in the distance, and Edgar leads his father off the stage.

SUMMARY

In this long and complex scene the following important events take place: The Lear plot and the Gloucester plot finally merge, as the two old men, each in direst wretchedness, meet. Lear, the more commanding figure of the two, is still eloquent in his madness, while Gloucester is just mutely unhappy. Gloucester's gullible superstition—which was played on for evil purposes by Edmund in Act I—here is played on by Edgar for the old man's own good. By tricking Gloucester into thinking he has escaped death from a great fall off a cliff, Edgar hopes to accomplish two things: convince Gloucester that the gods are on his side, thus bringing him out of his suicidal gloom; and give him the strength to recognize Edgar as his son.

The scene in which Edgar convinces Gloucester that he is on a steep cliff shows Edgar's poetic ingenuity at its finest. Edgar is no longer the gullible, easily fooled youth of the beginning of the play, but has become cunning and resourceful. Like Cordelia, he has matured considerably as a result of his terrible experiences in the world.

Lear, in his madness, is most magnificent in this scene. His mind seems to flit back and forth between reason and insanity, as Edgar observes. But beneath the wild banter, Lear, like the Fool in earlier scenes in the play, tells several home truths about life. His speech reveals his obsessions: how he mistook false court flattery in his youth for real respect and love; the general sexual rioting throughout all nature, for which Lear holds the female of the species most responsible, and which is continually upsetting any concept of law and order; the great injustices of the universe (a rich man gets away with the very crimes for which the poor are cruelly punished); his own former set of values which was false in that he was too much impressed with wealth, pomp and power, and ignored the humble and decent people of his kingdom; legitimacy of birth, which is no guarantee of decency of conduct; our own foreknowledge of grief—we somehow know when we are born that we are in for a life of folly and suffering, so that "the first time that we smell the air / We bawl and cry."

In his madness, Lear mistakes the guards who are trying to take him to Cordelia for enemy troops, and, with surprising strength, eludes them again.

Oswald shows several of his major characteristics in this, his final scene. He is completely, viciously unscrupulous. He is perfectly willing to slaughter the defenseless Gloucester for money and to please Regan, and, presumably, Goneril. He is prevented from doing this only by Edgar's presence. Oswald is also a snob; he feels that as a household servant and privileged messenger, it is below him to fight with a mere peasant, as Edgar ingeniously pretends to be. Yet, Oswald is still utterly loyal to Goneril. His dying words are a plea to his slayer to deliver the letter Goneril had given him to take to Edmund.

In the character of Oswald Shakespeare is showing that mere blind loyalty is not enough, when it is devoted to an evil person or cause. Thus Oswald becomes a commentary, 350 years after he was conceived, on the blind loyalty, say, of the Nazi petty functionaries who were "just doing their duty." For Shakespeare a man must decide for himself between right and wrong in every given instance and act accordingly. He must have the moral stamina to be disloyal to an evil master. An example of such virtue in the play is Cornwall's servant who slays him during the blinding of Gloucester.

The letter from Goneril to Edmund, now read by Edgar, places in writing the plot between the two to kill Albany and get married. Now Edgar, no longer gullible, finally knows everything about his evil brother.

ACT 4: SCENE 7

This great scene of the reunion of Cordelia and Lear takes place in Cordelia's tent in the French camp. Lear has evidently been recaptured by the attendants and has been returned to the camp, put to sleep, and dressed in fresh clothes while he slept. Cordelia tells Kent of her deep gratitude to him for all he has done for her father, begging him to come out of disguise and reveal himself to the others. Kent, however, asks her to wait until he thinks it is the proper time to show himself. Then Cordelia asks the doctor how her father is doing. The doctor says that since he has been sleeping soundly for a long time, they might wake him now. So Lear is borne in on a chair and placed before Cordelia, Kent and the doctor. Music is played to wake Lear as gently as possible, and Cordelia, staring at her father's sleeping face, reflects in wonder that her two sisters could have mistreated him. "Was this a face / To be oppos'd against the warring winds?" she asks, and makes the observation, made so often before in the play, that "Mine enemy's dog, / Though he had bit me, should have stood that night [of the storm] / Against my fire." Cordelia is amazed that her father was able to survive the experience at all.

As Lear begins to awaken, the doctor bids Cordelia speak to him. She asks her father how he is, but Lear, still half asleep, thinks she is "a soul in bliss" descended from heaven to mock him in hell, where he is "bound / Upon a wheel of fire, that mine own tears / Do scald like molten lead." When Cordelia asks him if he knows her, Lear repeats that she is a spirit, and asks in turn when she died. Finally Lear is fully awake. He is overcome with guilt when he confronts the daughter he has wronged and who, he thinks, still hates him. He tries to kneel before her for forgiveness, but Cordelia begs him to get up. Lear confesses tragically that "I am a very foolish fond old man, / Fourscore and upward, not an hour more or less; / And, to deal plainly, / I fear I am not in my perfect mind." He begs Cordelia not to weep, but says that if she has poison for him, he will drink it. He is sure she does not love him because he has wronged her, and her sisters, who benefited from him, hate him. "You have some cause" to hate me, Lear says, "they have not." But with simple nobility Cordelia assures him, "No cause, no cause." Then Lear asks her if he is in France, and Cordelia assures him he is in his own kingdom. Again Lear thinks he is being mocked. The doctor intervenes, telling Cordelia that Lear ought to rest again; he is still too weak to learn the whole history of where he is and how he got there. Lear, repeating that he is "old and foolish," leaves with Cordelia, the doctor and some attendants.

This immensely touching scene ends with a brief discussion between Kent and the Gentleman about the death of Cornwall and Edmund's taking the title of Earl of Gloucester. The Gentleman, not knowing who Kent is, mentions a rumor that Edgar and Kent are together in Germany. Kent evasively answers that rumors are not to be trusted; what is to be done now is to arm properly against the oncoming armies of Albany and Cornwall.

SUMMARY

This is one of the most moving scenes in the play because it deals with the emotionally charged reunion of Lear and Cordelia in the simplest possible terms. It is the complete antidote to the poisonous atmosphere of greed, betrayal and generally monstrous behavior which has preceded it in the play. Each character seems transfigured in an almost holy light. Lear, when he awakes, although feeble, has come to a full understanding of himself. He realizes his disabilities: that he is over eighty years old and not in his right mind. The one thing bothering him at this point is the guilt he feels towards Cordelia. He knows he has wronged her and feels she must hate him even more than Goneril and Regan do.

Cordelia, however, is all forgiving, concerned only to see her father restored to health. Although her speeches are still brief and unflowery, they are immensely moving. Cordelia gets into trouble originally, in the first scene of the play, because she cannot speak her love for Lear. Yet a line like her "No cause, no cause" is deeply affecting precisely because it is not fancy or rhetorical, but obviously expresses genuine feeling.

Kent, ever loyal and trustworthy, wishes to remain anonymous until it is perfectly appropriate to reveal himself. The nobility of the scene is established in the opening dialogue between Cordelia and Kent, which is filled with gratitude and humility.

Lear's long rest has apparently cleared his mind sufficiently to recognize Cordelia, but he cannot bear up under too much discussion. Note the contrast in his words with her in this scene to those in Act I, Scene 1. He has learned to have some humility; she has lost her unwillingness to reveal her love for him.

KING LEAR
ACT 5

ACT 5: SCENE 1

After the brief interval of affection and forgiveness in Act IV, Scene 7, we are plunged once again into a scene of monstrous plotting and intrigue. The scene shifts to the British camp near Dover, where Edmund and Regan enter, accompanied by soldiers and a flourish of drums. Edmund asks an officer to find out whether Albany is still on their side or if he has deserted them, since "he's full of alteration / And self-reproving." When the officer leaves on his errand, Regan comments that Albany certainly is untrustworthy. Then she gets to the matter which most closely concerns her: Does Edmund in fact love her sister? Edmund answers cagily that he loves Goneril honorably, but to think that he has seduced her is unworthy of Regan. He assures her that they have not had an adulterous affair. Regan begs Edmund not to be "familiar" with Goneril, and Edmund reassures her that he cares equally little for Goneril and "the Duke her husband."

Albany and Goneril themselves arrive, also accompanied by soldiers, drums and flags. Goneril's first remark (made aside) on seeing Edmund once more, is that she would rather lose the battle than that Regan should get Edmund for herself. Then Albany informs Regan and Edmund that he has heard that Lear and Cordelia are reunited, along with "others whom the rigour of our state / Forc'd to cry out." He points out that the only reason he is there to help out in the fighting is that "France invades our land." Goneril and Edmund are all for making peace with Albany because they need his army. A council of war is decided upon, but Edmund holds back a moment. Then Goneril and Regan argue about who is going to remain outside with Edmund. Neither is willing to trust the other alone with him for a second. Meanwhile Edgar, still disguised, enters. He asks Albany if he may have a word with him alone. The others all leave the stage for their council of war.

Edgar now hands Albany the letter which was given him by Oswald. "Before you fight the battle," Edgar tells Albany, "ope this letter." The letter, we remember, contains the plot between Goneril and Edmund to slay Albany and then get married. If Albany should be successful in battle, Edgar tells him, he is to let a trumpet sound, and a champion will come who will give proof of what is in the letter. If Albany falls in the battle, of course, it won't matter. Albany tries to get Edgar to stay until Albany has read the letter, but Edgar says he must leave, and he does.

Edmund re-enters and tells Albany that he has been success-ful in his spying on the French camp, but that they must hurry off to battle. When Albany leaves to rally his troops, Edmund remains behind for another of his cynical, witty and unscru-pulous soliloquies. He has sworn his love to both Goneril and Regan, he says, and each is madly jealous of the other. "Which of them shall I take?" he asks himself. "Both? one? or neither?" One thing is certain: He can enjoy neither sister if the other remains alive. Coldly and cynically he weighs the advantages and disadvantages of each sister in his mind. The chief obstacle in his way right now is Albany. He will let Albany fight in the impending battle because he can use his army. If Albany is killed, then all is well. If he survives, let Goneril kill him. In any case, one thing is clear: The merciful treatment which Albany intends for Lear and Cordelia must be vetoed after the battle. Edmund is concerned only with defending his state, not with debating about it. No enemies can be left alive, and Lear and Cordelia, although they are not active enemies, would be a rallying point for the now numerous people in Britain who hate Edmund.

SUMMARY

Two parallel strands run through this scene: the military situ-ation and the sexual situation. The military situation is as follows: The army of Cornwall and Regan has been placed under Edmund's command, even though Edmund is only an earl, and Cornwall was and Albany is a duke. There is even some question as to whether Edmund is an earl, because his father, Gloucester, is not dead yet, but has only been branded a traitor by Cornwall and Regan. Edmund, however, is mainly worried about his ally, Albany, and how trustworthy he is. He knows that Albany is deeply sympathetic to Lear and Cordelia. Neither Edmund nor Regan is sure of Albany's loyalty. He is much weaker than his wife, Goneril, and so is constantly shifting between a desire to help Lear and Cordelia, and a sense of his duty to repel any foreign invasion of England.

Albany has received from Edgar the letter that was meant for Edmund, setting forth Goneril's plan for him to murder Albany and marry her. This is the letter that Oswald was bringing to Edmund when he was killed by Edgar.

Running parallel to the military situation is the sexual triangle, which at the moment stands as follows:

Goneril is in love with Edmund, but must somehow get Albany killed before she can marry him. Regan is also in love with Edmund and has the advantage of being a widow. Edmund can't make up his mind which sister to take. What always motivates him is pure, calculating ambition. He has no emotional concern for either sister and is rather flattered and amused at their constant, embittered struggle for him. Three things are certain to him at this point: He is not going to bother killing Albany. If the impending battle doesn't accomplish that, he will let Goneril kill her husband. Whichever sister he does marry, the remaining one will have to be killed. The major problem for Edmund at this point is to decide which sister can bring him the most power with the least trouble. Albany's plan for showing mercy to Lear and Cordelia once the French forces have been routed is no good as far as Edmund is concerned. Edmund is concerned only with expediency, not mercy. It is inexpedient to leave alive any possible rallying point for an opposition force. So Lear and Cordelia must die.

ACT 5: SCENE 2

This brief scene takes place on a field between the British and French camps. Lear, Cordelia and the French forces enter and quickly leave the stage for the battle, amid flourishes of trumpets and drums. Then Edgar enters, leading Gloucester. He tells his father to rest in the shade of a tree until the battle is over. All Gloucester can do for the cause is "pray that the right may thrive." Then Edgar also races off for the battle. Suddenly the trumpets sound again to announce the retreat of the French forces. Edgar dashes in to tell his father the bad news that Lear and his daughter have lost the battle and are taken prisoner. He begs Gloucester to seek shelter with him, but the old man hasn't the heart to wander any further. Gloomily he tells Edgar that "a man may rot even here." Why keep running from death when that is all he wants? But Edgar tries to cheer him up again, in terms of stoic philosophy: "Men must endure / Their going hence, even as their coming hither." He tells his father, "Ripeness is all." He convinces Gloucester of this truth, and together they leave for safety.

SUMMARY

Although this scene is very brief, it raises many problems. The battle seems too short, compared with all the preparations for it in the play. It also seems inadequately described, as it takes place offstage, and the French apparently lose it in barely a minute. One possible answer is that the King of France is away, having been called home on urgent business. A more important answer is that since none of the major characters in the play is a soldier, we are not really interested in how they behave in battle, as we are, say, with Macbeth or Mark Antony. We only need to know the result of the fight, not the manner in which it was fought. Still another reason for the brevity of the battle scene is that the sympathies of Shakespeare's audience were divided between Lear and Cordelia on the one side, and desire for a British victory on the other. Shakespeare thus is minimizing the embarrassing fact that Lear and Cordelia are on the side of Britain's traditional enemy, France.

Why does Edgar still express hope to his father after the forces of Albany and Cornwall have won the battle? The reason is that he is hoping Albany will read the damning letter which Edgar gave him in the preceding scene. Once he has done that and learned of his wife's treachery, Edgar thinks Albany will bring over his army to Lear's side and help the French army defeat Cornwall.

Edgar's statement to his father that "Ripeness is all" is one of the major philosophical lines in the play. It means that the only important thing about life is to become ripe, to reach some sort of fulfillment and maturity. Then death doesn't matter. We have, of course, no more to say about the time of our death than we do about the time of our birth. We are born and we die when we are ripe to do so, like everything else in nature. The point is to achieve philosophical maturity—man's "ripeness"—before we die. Here, as elsewhere in the play, Shakespeare is drawing on the philosophy of Montaigne, the great French sixteenth-century essayist, who says "that to philosophize is to learn how to die."

ACT 5: SCENE 3

The final scene of the play takes place in the British camp near Dover. Edmund enters, bringing with him Lear and Cordelia as prisoners. He orders a group of officers to take them away until it is decided what to do with them. Cordelia tells Lear that she doesn't care what happens to her, but is unhappy for him. She tries to comfort the old man by telling him that now they will be reunited with Goneril and Regan, but this is slim comfort, indeed, for Lear cannot bear to see his two evil daughters again. Instead, he is quite content to live out the rest of his days in prison with Cordelia, where, he says, "We two alone will sing like birds i' the' cage:/ When thou dost ask me blessing, I'll kneel down, / And ask of thee forgiveness." In the prison they will gossip about court life, "and pray, and sing, and tell old tales." They will be utterly removed from the cares of the world, from "who's in, who's out" in court politics.

Edmund harshly breaks in on Lear's idyllic picture of prison life, and again orders a guard to take the prisoners away. Lear finally comforts Cordelia, telling her that "Upon such sacrifices, my Cordelia, / The Gods themselves throw incense." (In other words, when human beings have suffered and sacrificed as nobly as they have done, the gods must worship them, instead of their worshipping the gods. There are two major interpretations of what Lear means by "sacrifices." A. C. Bradley says he means his own and Cordelia's renunciation of the world. G. L. Kittredge thinks Shakespeare means specifically the sacrifices Cordelia has made for Lear's sake.)

As Lear and Cordelia are taken away to prison by the guard, Edmund hands one of his captains a secret note to bring to the jail with them. The note orders that Lear and Cordelia be executed in prison. Even their last bit of happiness is to be denied them. Edmund feels he has the authority to issue this death warrant because he is commander-in-chief of the British army, in place of the dead Cornwall. Cordelia is to be hanged, and then the rumor will be spread that she committed suicide out of despair. Edmund is quite aware of the bloodthirstiness of his order. He prepares the captain for this cruel mission by telling him that "to be tender-minded / Does not become a sword." These are hard times, Edmund says, and a man must be prepared to act ruthlessly in them if he hopes to get ahead. The officer promises to carry out the order, and Edmund sends him off, asking him to "write happy" when the execution has been carried out.

Now, amid a flourish of trumpets and drums, Albany, Goneril, Regan and some soldiers enter. Albany congratulates Edmund on his "valiant strain" which won the day's victory. But then he asks him for the royal prisoners he has taken, "so to use them / As we shall find their merits and our safety / May equally determine." Edmund tells Albany that he has sent them to prison, but holds back the information that he has secretly ordered their execution. Instead he says they will be ready for trial tomorrow. He and the rest of the army are too tired from the battle to think about Lear and Cordelia right now.

Edmund's high-handed behavior in sending Lear and Cordelia to prison without consulting him irritates Albany, who reminds Edmund that he is merely a commander in the war, but not really Albany's equal as far as civil authority is concerned. Albany is, after all, a duke, while Edmund, even if he has a right to his father's title, which is dubious while Gloucester is still alive, would only be an earl. But Regan intercedes for the man she loves and tells Albany that since Edmund led the army in the dead Cornwall's place, he has every right to order things as he pleases. Now open warfare breaks out between Regan and Goneril over Edmund. So inflamed is Goneril at her sister's standing up for Edmund that she forgets that her own husband is present, and she passionately begins to insult Regan. Unaware that Goneril has secretly poisoned her (this happened offstage), Regan begins to feel the first symptoms in her stomach. She defiantly gives Edmund all her "soldiers, prisoners, patrimony," and calls him her "lord and master." Relations between the sisters and Edmund and Albany become very tense. Enjoying the onset of Regan's death agony, Goneril bitchily asks her, "Mean you to enjoy him [Edmund]?" Albany angrily reminds his wife that it is not up to her to decide whom Regan shall marry, and Edmund, who all this time has been cynically enjoying the fuss made over him, sides with Goneril and tells Albany it isn't up to him to decide either.

Finally, Albany can stand the squabble no longer. He has read the letter given him by Edgar in Act V, Scene 1, and his fury at the treachery of Goneril and Edmund has been growing ever since. Now he breaks into the argument to inform Edmund and Goneril that they are both under arrest for "capital treason." With bitter humor he tells Regan that her claim on Edmund is barred: Edmund is apparently already promised to Goneril. If Regan wants to marry again, Albany tells her, she will have to marry him, for his lady has first claim on Edmund. Goneril laughs off Albany's bitter sarcasm, calling it "an interlude," i.e., a little bit of farcical drama, like a short comedy. Ignoring his wife, Albany challenges Edmund to a duel. He calls for the trumpet to sound, as Edgar had told him to do when he gave him the letter. Then, throwing down his glove in the standard gesture of challenge, he tells Edmund that if a champion does not appear to fight him, he will lower himself to duel with him. Edmund throws down his glove, too, and replies that he will maintain his "truth and honour firmly" against anybody. Meanwhile the effects of the poison Goneril gave Regan have been increasing, and now, feeling mortally sick, Regan is led into Albany's tent.

A herald enters, sounds the trumpet, and reads the following proclamation: "If any man of quality or degree within the lists of the army will maintain upon Edmund, supposed Earl of Gloucester that he is a manifold traitor, let him appear by the third sound of the trumpet." Three times the trumpet is blown, and on the third call it is answered by Edgar's trumpet. Edgar enters, fully armed, his face concealed behind a visor. The herald asks him who he is, what his rank is, and why he has come to answer the summons. Edgar replies that his "name is lost" but that he is of noble blood, as noble as his adversary's. Then, calling Edmund "False to thy gods, thy brother, and thy father," Edgar challenges him to combat as a "toad-spotted traitor." Edmund replies coolly that according to the rules of knighthood, he ought to demand his challenger's name, but since the stranger seems well bred and warlike, he will consent to fight him.

The two brothers duel, and Edmund eventually falls, mortally wounded. Albany calls for a doctor to save him (because he wants Edmund to live long enough to be tried for treason), and Goneril cries out that he should not have fought because the laws of chivalry do not require a noble to fight "an unknown opposite." But Albany abruptly tells her, "Shut your mouth, dame," or he will stuff it with the incriminating letter he has. He even tries to get the dying Edmund to read the letter. After exchanging insults with her husband, Goneril leaves the stage, followed by an officer sent by Albany because he fears what she may do in her desperation.

Now Edmund, in his death agony, confesses to all the charges brought against him. Indeed, he says he is guilty of "more, much more; the time will bring it out." (Presumably Edmund means his secret order to execute Lear and Cordelia. Why he doesn't send a messenger to stop the execution at this point, when he does later, is a mystery in the play.) Then Edmund asks Edgar again who he is, saying that he forgives him if he is a nobleman. Now is the time that Edgar decides finally to reveal himself. "My name is Edgar," he says proudly, lifting the visor, "and thy father's son. / The Gods are just, and of our pleasant vices / Make instruments to plague us." He adds that Gloucester had to pay with his eyes for begetting Edmund in a "dark and vicious place," i.e., illegitimately. Albany embraces Edgar and wants to know where he managed to hide himself all this time, and how he knew of the miseries of his father. Edgar tells the story of his disguise as Tom of Bedlam and of his nursing the blinded Gloucester. He didn't reveal himself to his father until just a half hour ago, he says, and he did it then only because he wasn't sure that he would survive the combat with Edmund. When he told Gloucester who he was, and asked for his blessing, the old man's "flaw'd heart, / Alack, too weak the conflict to support! / Twixt two extremes of passion, joy and grief, / Burst smilingly." Albany and even Edmund are moved by the story of Gloucester's final reconciliation with his son and his ensuing death. Edgar goes on to tell how he met with the banished Kent and joined forces with him.

Edgar's tale is interrupted by the frantic entrance of a Gentleman, carrying a bloody knife. The Gentleman tells Albany that the knife is hot from the heart of Goneril, who stabbed herself after poisoning her sister. Both are now dead. Edmund comments, with typical wit, even in his death throes: "I was contracted to them both: all three / Now marry in an instant." Edmund also expresses here perhaps the only genuine emotion he has had throughout the play: "Yet Edmund was belov'd." This suggests that his whole vicious career may have been caused by his feeling that he wasn't loved, a feeling relieved here by the death of the two sisters for love of him. Albany's attitude, however, is that their death was the judgment of heaven, for which he can't feel any pity. At this point Kent enters, seeking Lear. Albany remembers that he doesn't know where Lear and Cordelia are. But before anything can be done about it, the bodies of Goneril and Regan are brought onstage. Edmund tells Kent what happened, and then decides, since he is dying, to do at least one good deed in his life. He tells Albany of his secret execution warrant and bids him send a messenger to prevent the deaths of Lear and Cordelia. Albany does so, and the dying Edmund is borne offstage.

But Edmund's last bit of mercy comes too late, for now Lear enters, with the dead Cordelia in his arms. Howling with horror, Lear begs for a looking glass to see if Cordelia has any breath of life left in her. He places the glass to her lips and convinces himself that she does still breath. He is too absorbed in trying to revive Cordelia to notice that Kent has knelt by his side to reveal himself to his King at last. Although later he does recognize Kent, at this moment Lear has no mind for anything but his Cordelia, whom he begs to "stay a little." Of her he says, "Her voice was ever soft, / Gentle and low, an excellent thing in woman." (And very different from the shrill, grating, fishwife voices of Goneril and Regan heard earlier in this scene.) Then Lear remembers that in a last surge of royal power he had killed the executioner who was hanging Cordelia. An officer confirms this story of Lear's last heroic action. Kent, Albany and Edgar try to tell Lear the bits of the story that he doesn't know, but his mind has completely gone now, in sorrow for Cordelia. Even the announcement by an officer that Edmund has just died causes Albany to say, "That's but a trifle here," in the face of the overwhelming tragedy of Cordelia's death and Lear's final suffering. Lear gazes raptly at his daughter, trying to convince himself that there is still a stir of life in her. "Why should a dog, a horse, a rat, have life, / And thou no breath at all?" he asks bitterly. Finally, the majestic old King begs someone to undo a button that is constricting him, and, with a final hope that Cordelia may yet be alive, dies of a broken heart.

Edgar tries to revive him, but Kent wisely says: "Vex not his ghost: O! let him pass; he hates him / That would upon the rack of this tough world / Stretch him out longer." The wonder, Kent says, is that he managed to endure so long. Albany commands that the body of Lear be borne away and asks Kent and Edgar to rule the kingdom. But Kent refuses: He is too brokenhearted at the death of his master, who he says calls him. Edgar will rule alone. The final words of the play, given in some editions to Albany, and in others to Edgar, aptly summarize, whoever speaks them, the feelings of the survivors:

The weight of this sad time we must obey; / Speak what we feel, not what we ought to say. / The oldest hath borne most: we that are young / Shall never see so much, nor live so long.

Then the survivors leave the stage, to the solemn music of a funeral march.

SUMMARY

In this titanic final scene, one of the richest in the play in action, passion and poetry, all the tangled threads of the drama are tied together. Lear and Cordelia, in their imprisonment and death, reach their highest peaks of grandeur. Completely forgiving each other and prepared to renounce the world, they desire at the beginning of the scene only to be left in peace together in prison. But even this small mercy is denied them by the cold, ambitious villainy of Edmund. He does repent, on the point of his own death, but it is too late to save Lear and Cordelia.

Lear's death is foreshadowed by that of Gloucester, who also dies of a broken heart. Each has been restored to his one loving child, but in both cases it is too late. It is significant that Gloucester's death occurs offstage. We are only told about it by Edgar so that it won't detract us from the death of Lear. For although Gloucester is like the King in situation, he is a much shallower and more superficial man, incapable of the poetic grandeur of feeling which Lear expresses.

Edgar's challenge and duel with his brother Edmund show how far he has progressed from the gullible, ineffectual young man who was tricked into fighting a mock duel to further Edmund's plot in Act II, Scene 1. All the ingenuity and stamina involved in his disguise as Tom of Bedlam, and, later, as the peasant who guides and protects his blinded father, now come into play. By the end he has indeed become a knight in shining armor, whom even Edmund must respect.

Edmund behaves in character throughout the last scene, allowing Goneril and Regan to fight over him, but then rather grandly accepting the challenge from the disguised Edgar. As he is dying, Edmund has two moments of glory: his jest about marrying both sisters in death, and his last-minute attempt to save Lear and Cordelia. Edmund is a very complex villain indeed.

Albany, like Edgar, has grown during the play. Where earlier he was overshadowed and somewhat henpecked by his ambitious, unscrupulous wife, here in the last scene he is in complete command.

Goneril and Regan, behaving to the last like the vicious animals they have been compared with throughout the play, meet their just ends. Goneril secretly poisons her sister and then stabs herself when it is evident that Albany knows of her treachery, has written proof of it, and will punish her for it. Not many tears are wasted on their deaths.

Kent, loyal to the end, finally reveals himself to Lear. He is unwilling to receive any power in the kingdom after Lear's death. In his loyalty he can think only of joining his King in death.

CHARACTER ANALYSES

KING LEAR

Lear is basically a generous and unsuspicious man, but he is too used to getting his own way after a long lifetime of absolute rulership. He is also hot tempered and self-willed. Despite his age he is in top physical condition at the beginning of the play (he goes out hunting when he is staying with Goneril). His disinheriting of Cordelia is not an act of senility but the act of a man who will stand no opposition to his slightest whim. What the opening scene does prove is that he lacks common sense and insight into people and that he puts too much faith in outward show. He seems to have known enough about his daughters before to have preferred Cordelia to the others, but his folly consists in his accepting at face value the hypocritical protestations of love by Goneril and Regan.

Lear is like a man who wants to eat his cake and also have it. Having given away his kingdom, he expects to retain the dignity and power of kingship and refuses to accept a lesser role in life. This first scene, however, is the only one in the play in which Lear is shown in an unsympathetic light. Immediately afterward, when he goes to stay with Goneril, his suffering begins. It is so intense that we can only sympathize with him. We learn, too, that Lear has attracted the intense fidelity and devotion of Cordelia, Gloucester, Kent, the Fool and, later, Albany. He must have had good qualities to do so. Hurt deeply by his daughters' ingratitude, Lear throughout the play is desperately fighting a losing battle with madness. He is determined to remain "every inch a king." His deep-rooted pride will not allow him to diminish his retinue by one knight. He would rather go out into the storm. There, as his trials increase in intensity, a transformation seems to overtake Lear. He loses his temper less and less and begins to learn patience and humility. His suffering makes him aware of the suffering of all humanity—something he had been protected from by court flattery when he was a King. There is also a streak of self-pity in the Lear of the first half of the play. He feels himself "a man more sinned against than sinning," and keeps reminding his daughters that he "gave them all." This self-pity, too, is purged from his character, and he comes to realize that the world owes him nothing. In his madness, Lear comes paradoxically to a true vision of the workings of the universe and of man's place in it. He rebels, with puritanical disgust, against the lust, greed and hypocrisy which run the world. Toward the end of the play, under the love of Cordelia and the care of her physician, Lear achieves a degree of serenity until the final blow—the death of Cordelia—deprives him of all reason for living.

GLOUCESTER

Like Lear, Gloucester is an old, white-haired man, a widower, whose children are still comparatively young. He, too, has been guilty of folly and injustice. He, too, is normally affectionate, but overhasty in his actions. Like Lear, he cannot distinguish between his good child and his wicked one. His son Edmund, as a bastard, is an embarrassment to Gloucester, and he keeps him away from court for several years. But then, when Edmund returns to court, Gloucester is all too willing to believe his slander against Edgar. He is far more superstitious and credulous than Lear. In fact, he is the only completely superstitious character in the play, giving great credence to such things as eclipses and the movement of the stars as forces in human behavior. He is also a very weak, though good-hearted man. Although he disapproves of what Cornwall and Regan are doing to Lear and although they are doing it in Gloucester's own castle, all he can do is chide them for it; he can't stop them. This is partly because he is only an earl, whereas Cornwall is a duke. But partly it is because Gloucester doesn't have the strength of character necessary to put a stop to rampant evil. His life, too, has been more devoted to the enjoyment of sensual pleasure than Lear's, as the begetting of the illegitimate Edmund shows. In his suffering, Gloucester seems like Lear, but not nearly so impressive. He tends more to whimper than to lash out at his oppressors as Lear does in his great biblical tirades. His blinding by Cornwall makes him pessimistic to the brink of suicide. Even then he is gullible, believing Edgar's story that he is on the brink of the cliffs of Dover, instead of simply on level ground. It is harder for Gloucester to learn what Lear and Edgar know: that a man must endure whatever horrors the fates may heap on his shoulders. He doesn't have to grin and bear it, but he must bear it.

GONERIL

Lear's oldest daughter is a supremely evil woman. She understands her father very well and plays up to him with her hypocritical avowal of love in the first scene. But she knows that he is willful and changeable and decides to play him for all that she can get. She knows, too, that Cordelia has always been Lear's favorite and is jealous of her, as Edmund is jealous of Edgar. She is highly intelligent, but has no sense of proportion. She despises her husband, Albany, for being weaker willed than she is, but fails to see that if he is, it is a sense of decency which makes him so. She fails utterly to see Lear's inherent nobility. She is also very thick-skinned and callous. It doesn't bother her that her bargaining with Lear about how many knights he is to retain is for him the most inhuman degradation. His justifiable tirades against her just slip off her like water off a duck's back. She is determined to reduce Lear to beggary, to utter dependence on her charity for the means to live, and doesn't care about the devastating psychological effect such an attitude would have on a man used to being an absolute ruler all his life. Her "love" for Edmund is pure lust for sex and power. It is based on Edmund's handsome exterior and on his temperamental likeness to herself. He, too, will stop at nothing to get his way. Far more ambitious and unscrupulous than Albany, Edmund appeals to Goneril as the kind of man who is worthy of her.

REGAN

Like her older sister, Regan is intelligent, grasping and cruel. The only thing she lacks is initiative. She is always following Goneril's footsteps, sometimes even outdoing her in cruelty, but never originating anything. Typical of Regan is her remark when Cornwall orders that Kent be placed in the stocks until noon. "Till noon!" Regan exclaims, "Till night, my lord; and all night too." She is always going others one better in cruelty, but she doesn't poison anybody, commit adultery or plot against her husband's life, as Goneril does. She is presumably more "happily married" than Goneril because her husband, Cornwall, is just as vicious and strong willed as she is. She even slays the servant who kills Cornwall. Nevertheless, when Cornwall is killed, Regan immediately transfers her affections to Edmund, for the same reasons that Goneril loves him. Regan shamelessly throws all her possessions at Edmund after he wins the battle against France. It is typical of Goneril's power over Regan, however, that it is Goneril who poisons Regan and not the other way around.

CORDELIA

The youngest sister is almost like the Virgin Mary in her meekness and gentleness. As good as her sisters are evil, Cordelia is a unique portrait in literature. Only Shakespeare could draw a picture of such utter goodness in so few lines and not become sentimental. Although Cordelia is present in only four of the twenty-six scenes of the play, we never forget her during the long stretch when she is offstage. Her character is based on three traits: reverence, pity and absolute devotion to the truth. It is this latter trait which gets her into trouble at the beginning of the play. She lacks her sisters' hypocrisy, but is too severe and unyielding in her insistence on telling Lear the truth. She tells him, "I love your Majesty / According to my bond; no more no less." This shows that although Cordelia had always been Lear's favorite daughter, she understands him as little as he does her, and much less than Goneril and Regan understand him. During the course of the play, the two come to a mutual understanding, and Cordelia learns the same lesson of humility that Lear must learn. She is married to the King of France at the beginning of the play and is able to arouse enough love in him for him to take her without a dowry and to bring his whole army to Dover to re-establish her father on his throne. She also has aroused intense devotion in Kent, who gets himself exiled for speaking out in her favor, and in the Fool, who pines away for her when she is in exile. When she is reunited with her father, she looks out anxiously for his welfare, and assures him of her undying devotion to him in words of noble simplicity. Most critics and spectators of *Lear* find Cordelia's death the most unbearably poignant episode in the play.

EDGAR

Edgar undergoes one of the most marked developments of any character in *King Lear*. At the beginning he is as credulous as his father, Gloucester. It is ridiculously easy for Edmund to fool him. He cannot suspect evil because he is wholly good himself. Also, Edgar is the most religious character in the play, who believes that the gods are always just. Edgar learns, however, to be resourceful and ingenious in order to survive. He adopts the disguise of Tom of Bedlam because he knows that since nobody will take a mad beggar seriously, he will be able to survive while Edmund is plotting against him. Later, his disguise as a peasant is good enough to fool even his own father. He learns to be cheerful in adversity and helpful in a practical way. When the Fool drops out of the play, it is up to Edgar to cheer and comfort Lear and look after his welfare. He is reliable, and the state is in good hands with him at the end of the play. By the time of his duel with Edmund, he has become a strong, self-reliant man. He is still deeply good, sometimes even priggish, as when he tells Edmund that Gloucester was blinded because of his "pleasant vices." Edgar is no longer taken in by evil, and yet has not become hard-hearted or cynical.

EDMUND

Edmund is the complete opposite of his brother. Where Edgar is religious, Edmund is a complete atheist and materialist. He believes that men just use the gods as excuses for their own bad behavior. "Thou, Nature, art my goddess," he proudly proclaims, meaning that he thinks of himself as a natural man, not bound by any moral or ethical considerations. The gods are to Edmund merely "an admirable evasion of whore-master man, to lay his goatish disposition to the charge of a star!" Edmund is highly intelligent. He plots coldly and brilliantly to gain first his brother's inheritance, then his father's title, and finally the entire kingdom. He is, in short, an ambitious adventurer. He lets nothing stand in his way. He even betrays his father to his enemies. Although Edmund is physically handsome, he suffers deeply from the fact of his illegitimacy and the mockery he has had to endure because of it. At the very beginning of the play his being a bastard is discussed in his presence, with cynical wit by his father and Kent. In his first soliloquy he reflects, "Why bastard? Wherefore base? / When my dimensions are as well compact, / My mind as generous, and my shape as true, as honest madam's issue?" Then, thinking over his plot, he concludes, "I grow, I prosper; / Now, gods, stand up for bastards!" Edmund's psychological suffering for being a bastard provides him with at least a speck of motivation for his evil in the play. Other sympathetic aspects of Edmund are his subtle humor and his refusal to fool himself. He says, while dying, of Goneril and Regan, "I was contracted to them both: all three / Now marry in an instant," and we feel a pang of sympathy for him when he says, "Yet Edmund was belov'd." Also, at the point of death he tries to save Lear and Cordelia from his own cruel death warrant. In these ways, Edmund is a much more appealing villain than Cornwall, but he is still a coldly calculating villain, much like Iago in *Othello,* or Richard III. The one thing his intelligence fails to comprehend is that evil is self-defeating, a failure of comprehension that is his destruction.

KENT

The key to Kent's character is his absolute devotion to Lear. An old man, although not as old as Lear or Gloucester, Kent puts himself to endless trouble to be with Lear and to help him whenever he can. What makes his behavior all the more admirable is that since Lear banished him in the first scene for defending Cordelia, Kent is in England on pain of death, should he be recognized and captured. Hence he must maintain his disguise throughout. He is blunt and eccentric, utterly lacking any of the smoothness and suavity of the usual courtier. He is a plain, honest man, who, like Lear, acts hotly and rashly. To Cornwall he is merely "some fellow / Who, having been prais'd for bluntness, doth affect / A saucy roughness"—in other words, he is putting his bluntness on. But this is untrue. Kent simply cannot control his temper when he sees the ingratitude and injustice of Lear's daughters or the lack of respect for Lear that Oswald shows. He is the typical warrior, rather than courtier: unthinking, hot tempered, but profoundly loyal and unselfish. He is also a fatalist. When he is placed in the stocks and there is nothing more he can do, he simply says, "Fortune good night; / Smile once more, turn thy wheel!" and promptly goes to sleep. His devotion to Lear is such that when Lear dies and Kent is offered a share in ruling the kingdom, he refuses, because "My master calls me, I must not say no." In short, he must die, too, once Lear is dead.

THE FOOL

Another devoted servant of Lear's. In happier days he entertained the king and court with his quips and riddles. When we first see him, he is unhappy because his favorite, Cordelia, has been exiled. He alternately cheers and torments Lear with his witty insights into Lear's folly and the ingratitude of his daughters. Like Kent, he cannot be separated from Lear, but he is not so brave as the old warrior. Goneril and Regan stun him into silence, and he is so terrified of the storm that Kent has to comfort him. The Fool has true insight into what is going on in the world, but he is also more than a touch

insane. This is part of the convention of court jesters, however, and is not original with Shakespeare's Fool. The Fool is
someone who is so far outside the realms of political and
social power that he is privileged to make any comments on
his superiors that he chooses, as long as he is witty and amus-
ing. In Lear, the Fool sings songs, speaks in puns and riddles,
and is often rather difficult to understand. He is apparently
quite young, and the suffering he has endured and seen around
him has been too much for him. He disappears mysteriously
halfway through the play, after he has taught Lear all he can
about the ways of the world.

ALBANY

A vacillating man, but not nearly so weak as Goneril thinks
him. It merely takes him a long time to make up his mind
because he is the kind of man who has to weigh allegiances
very carefully. Albany at first doesn't interfere with Goneril's
cruel treatment of Lear, and Lear makes no distinction
between him and Cornwall. He is obviously in love with his
wife for her physical beauty. But as the play progresses,
Albany's essential decency emerges. He cannot bear the
cruelty that has been shown Lear, and at the risk of losing his
wife to Edmund he defends the old King. He roundly
upbraids Goneril as "Most barbarous, most degenerate," and
when he hears that his brother-in-law Cornwall was slain while
gouging out Gloucester's eyes, Albany cries out in exultation:
"This shows you are above, / You justicers, that these our
nether crimes / So speedily can venge!" Nevertheless, Albany
is a patriotic man, and leads his troops in the war against the
French although he must fight on Edmund's side against Lear
and Cordelia. He is a man who can be pushed around only so
far, and when he learns of Goneril's plot to have him killed
and to marry Edmund, he has the plotters arrested for treason. He has learned that there is no compromise with evil.

CORNWALL

Cornwall seems at first to be as much under Regan's thumb as

Albany is under Goneril's. It soon becomes obvious, however, that Cornwall is at least the equal of the sisters in cruelty. He thinks nothing of putting Kent in the stocks for insulting Oswald, taking over Gloucester's castle completely, siding with Regan against Lear and even locking Lear out in the storm. Cornwall's crowning moment of villainy comes when he gouges out Gloucester's eyes with his own thumbs. It is for this last outrageous deed that Cornwall's own servant stabs him (an unheard of act in those days). As another servant says, "I'll never care what wickedness I do / If this man come to good." Regan wastes no time mourning for him, and neither do we.

OSWALD

Oswald, like Kent, is fiercely loyal, but to the wrong person. He will do anything for Goneril. But unlike Kent, instead of being blunt and outspoken, Oswald is an oily and suave snob, which is why Kent despises him. When Oswald speaks disrespectfully to Lear at Goneril's house, Kent immediately trips him up and sends him sprawling for his insolence. Later, at Gloucester's castle, Kent rightly calls Oswald "a lily-livered . . . super-serviceable, finical rogue," and "a knave, beggar, coward, pandar, and the son and heir of a mongrel bitch." Oswald is loyal, however, and even performs Goneril's evil missions with more zest than is necessary because he has a taste for cruelty himself. His loyalty is shown when Regan tries to worm out of him the contents of the letter he is carrying from Goneril to Edmund. He steadfastly refuses to let her see it. His cruelty is shown by his willingness to stab the defenseless Gloucester in the back. When he is prevented from doing so by Edgar, disguised as a peasant, Oswald, the complete snob, is insulted that a social inferior should dare to fight him. But his final action is a loyal one: He begs Edgar to deliver the letter with which he had been entrusted. Oswald is the kind of man who might have been decent if he had attached himself to a decent master, but with no conscience of his own, he is a complete villain in the pay of a Goneril.

FRANCE

The King of France is a generous, intelligent man, who sees enough in Cordelia to be willing to marry her without a dowry. He goes to immense trouble to launch an invasion of England in order to rescue Lear. But then he makes a fatal mistake by returning to France just before the battle because of urgent business at home. By leaving his army in the command of a marshal, he may have forfeited the victory. His motives in landing an army at Dover are completely honorable. He desires no territorial conquest, but merely to see Cordelia happy again.

THE DUKE OF BURGUNDY

We see Burgundy only briefly in the first scene. He is the other suitor for Cordelia's hand. Apparently he has priority over France, but he loses out on marrying Cordelia because he is too cold and materialistic to wed her without a dowry. France puns on his name and character by calling him "wat'rish Burgundy." Even Lear doesn't seem to think much of him in the scene, although he has no sympathy for Cordelia either, then.

THE PHYSICIAN

A quiet, obedient and intelligent practitioner, the physician realizes that the only hope of restoring Lear to a degree of sanity is to let him rest after his great travail. "Our foster-nurse of nature is repose," he says, "The which he lacks; that to provoke in him, / Are many simples operative, whose power / Will close the eye of anguish." The physician probably represents the best Elizabethan medical practice. He intelligently asks Cordelia to be the first to speak to Lear when he awakens, and his idea of awakening Lear to the sound of music is highly interesting because this was the way in which the essayist Montaigne, who greatly influenced Shakespeare, used to be awakened. He very much resembles the doctor in *Macbeth*.

OTHER MINOR CHARACTERS

Other minor characters, with the exception of Curan, Edmund's servant, tend like the physician to be good, simple men. The Gentleman who keeps Kent abreast of latest developments and Cornwall's servants who revolt against their master and try to comfort the blinded Gloucester are humble, decent men who do much, in their small ways, to offset the aggressive evil of half the major characters.

CRITICAL COMMENTARY

In 1681 Nahum Tate, a popular hack playwright of the day, and the poet laureate of England, undertook to revise *King Lear* on the theory that it was "a Heap of Jewels, unstrung and unpolisht." He completely rewrote the play, giving it a happy ending, with Lear, Gloucester and Cordelia all surviving and Edgar marrying Cordelia and ruling Britain happily forever after. Tate's version held the stage until 1838, when the great actor, Macready, restored the original text throughout. If Tate's revision seems absurd to us today, it may be because the extremes of human cruelty which he glossed over have become everyday realities in the twentieth century. Given the evil forces set in motion at the beginning of *Lear,* we are unable to imagine any less tragic an outcome than Shakespeare provides.

This was not always the case, however. Even so eminent a critic as Samuel Johnson approved, in his edition of *Lear,* the Tate version, saying, "the publick has decided. Cordelia, from the time of Tate, has always retired with victory and felicity. And, if my sensations could add any thing to the general suffrage, I might relate, that I was many years ago so shocked by Cordelia's death, that I know not whether I ever endured to read again the last scenes of the play till I undertook to revise them as an editor." The death of Cordelia does indeed strike most readers of Lear as gratuitous and unnecessary. After all, if Edmund had remembered just a moment earlier to cancel his death warrant, she might have been spared. During his long death scene Edmund has several opportunities to remember, but never seems to get around to stopping the fatal order. Also, the audience often feels that Lear has suffered more than enough in the play. Couldn't he be allowed to die happy in prison with his daughter, or, with Edgar's victory over Edmund, spend his last days with Cordelia in the comfort of her home? To feel this way is to miss the point, however. By allowing Cordelia to die, and then, very soon after, Lear, Shakespeare seems to be saying that only in death can we achieve peace, that to continue to live in the world of King Lear is no blessing, and that tragic and evil things do often happen by mere chance. Charles Lamb, the great early nineteenth-century critic and essayist, answered Dr. Johnson and paved the way for dropping the Tate version of Lear when he indignantly wrote, in 1811: "A happy ending!—as if the living martyrdom that Lear had gone through,—the flaying of his feelings alive, did not make a fair dismissal from the stage of life the only decorous thing for him. If he is to live and be happy after, if he could sustain this world's burden after, why all this pudder and preparation,—why torment us with all this unnecessary sympathy? As if the childish pleasure of getting his gilt robes and sceptre again could tempt him to act over again his misused station,—as if at his years, and with his experience, anything was left but to die."

Lamb also made the famous statement that "Lear is essentially impossible to be represented on a stage. . . . to see Lear acted, —to see an old man tottering about the stage with a walking stick, turned out of doors by his daughters in a rainy night, has nothing in it but what is painful and disgusting. We want to take him into shelter and relieve him. That is all the feeling which the acting of Lear ever produced in me. But the Lear of Shakespeare cannot be acted. The contemptible machinery by which they mimic the storm which he goes out in, is not more inadequate to represent the horrors of the real elements, than any actor can be to represent Lear: they might more easily propose to personate the Satan of Milton upon a stage, or one of Michael Angelo's terrible figures. The greatness of Lear is not in corporeal dimension, but in intellectual: the explosions of his passion are terrible as a volcano: they are storms turning up and disclosing to the bottom that sea, his mind, with all its vast riches. It is his mind which is laid bare." Lamb preferred to read Shakespeare alone in his study, letting his imagination do the work which no amount of mechanical stagecraft can perform.

A later nineteenth-century critic, A. C. Bradley, said that although *Lear* is Shakespeare's greatest work, it is not the best of his plays, nor is it the most popular of the four great tragedies—*Hamlet, Othello, Lear* and *Macbeth*—with audiences. Bradley goes further than Lamb in maintaining that "its comparative unpopularity is due, not merely to the extreme painfulness of the catastrophe, but in part to its dramatic defects. . . ." What are these defects? They are summarized by Kenneth Muir in his Introduction to the New Arden edition of King Lear: "that Edgar would be unlikely to write to Edmund when he could speak with him, and that Gloucester would have noticed the improbability; that Gloucester had no need to go to Dover for the purpose of committing suicide; and that it is strange that he should show no surprise when Edgar drops into dialect during his encounter with Oswald; that there is no good reason why Edgar should not reveal himself to his father, or why Kent should preserve his disguise until the last scene; that Edmund, after he has received his fatal wound, delays unnecessarily in telling of the danger to Lear and Cordelia; and that it is absurd for Edgar to return from his hiding-place to soliloquize in his father's castle." Reasonable answers to all these points can be found in defense of Shakespeare's dramatic technique, but they are beside the point, because in *King Lear* Shakespeare is dealing with an unreasonable, irrational world. It is a world which includes the animal savagery of a Cornwall gouging out Gloucester's eyes, and the divine compassion of a Cordelia forgiving the father who has wronged her. It is a world of primitive terror such as strikes the outcasts on the heath during the storm, and of the utmost sophistication as in Edmund's witty, dialectical soliloquies. In short, it is our world, and, as G. Wilson Knight points out, "The tragedy is most poignant in that it is purposeless, unreasonable. It is the most fearless artistic facing of the ultimate cruelty of things in our literature."

Most modern critics have been willing to assume that if Shakespeare had wanted to knit *King Lear* into a "well-made play," he was quite capable of doing so. They have taken the vagueness of the chronology of the play (no one knows when any individual scene takes place) and the vagueness of the geography (where is Gloucester's castle?) to mean that Shakespeare deliberately wanted such points vague, thus universalizing the meaning of the play. Thus Lear's tragedy is not the tragedy of a specific, actual old King of Britain, but of every old man, and the corrupt court surrounding him is not so much a commentary on court politics in ancient Britain as on all political bodies. What the modern critic is most concerned with is the imagery of *Lear*. Why, as one industrious reader of the play has pointed out, are there 133 separate mentions of 64 different animals in the play? As Bradley shows in illustration, "Goneril is a kite: her ingratitude has a serpent's tooth: she has struck her father most serpent-like upon the very heart: her visage is wolvish: she has tied sharp-toothed unkindness like a vulture on her father's breast," and so on for most of the characters in the play. The answer seems to be in Albany's lines, that "Humanity must perforce prey on itself / Like monsters of the deep" if man will persist in letting his animal appetites go unchecked. Or, in Muir's words, "This imagery is partly designed to show man's place in the Chain of Being, and to bring out the sub-human nature of the evil characters, partly to show man's weakness compared with the animals, and partly to compare human existence to the life of the jungle."

Caroline Spurgeon, a pioneer in the reading of Shakespeare's plays according to their dominant images, finds the central image of *Lear* to be that "of a human body in anguished movement, tugged, wrenched, beaten, pierced, stung, scourged, dislocated, flayed, gashed, scalded, tortured, and finally broken on the rack." We see the truth of her interpretation in the scene in which Lear wakes up to find Cordelia at his side, and says "I am bound / Upon a wheel of fire, that mine own tears / Do scald like molten lead." Then, later, the same image of medieval torture is evoked by Kent, who tells

Edgar, "O! let him pass; he hates him / That would upon the rack of this tough world / Stretch him out longer." Such references are more than coincidence. A point is being made through them about the nature of the world and because there are so many, their cumulative effect "expresses the suffering not only of Lear, but of man. . . ."

Robert B. Heilman, in *This Great Stage: Image and Structure in* "King Lear" (1947; reprinted 1963) finds the significance of *King Lear* in a series of recurrent and related images which reinforce the theme that is "intellectual conquest and salvation through imaginative vision." Lear acted on rationalistic principles, not imaginative vision when he divided his kingdom. He suffers from "wrong imagination." Through the suffering of his madness, he experiences "an imaginative awakening" in which he understands what the true values are. Similarly, Gloucester at the beginning of the play is deficient in insight; he "does not ask enough questions," but he learns the spiritual truth that he must "bear / Affliction till it do cry out itself / 'Enough, enough.'" With the fact that Lear learns true reason in his madness, Heilman associates the Fool and Edgar. "Shakespeare takes three very 'unlikely specimens,' as the world might view them, a crazy old man long told that he is in his dotage, a Fool who may be clever but is probably unbalanced and is certainly a no-account, a naive young man who manages so ill that he can save himself only by becoming an outcast bedlam—and makes them, as far as the reflective and imaginative world is concerned, his three wise men." Lear's symbolic patterns, the Fool's shrewd remarks, Edgar's "gnomic observations" constitute a commentary on experience of human life. Heilman notes that this commentary comes from "the humbled, the scorned and the exiled" from the "humble and meek" whom Christian tradition has exalted.

Contrasted with this group, which finds truth and wisdom in madness, Heilman sees the evil group, Goneril, Regan, and Edmund, finding "madness in reason." All three are rationalists and apply what seems to them the standards of common sense. He shows that both Goneril and Regan like and use the words "wisdom" and "wise" when they describe conduct which is to their self-interest. They view Lear's state of mind (at the end of Act I) rationally and analytically, noting that he "hath ever but slenderly known himself." In accordance with what they observe, they lay their plans to deprive him of his symbols of status. They reason only from need—values such as dignity they deny. (Lear protests this when he cries "O, reason not the need.") They both agree that Lear must learn the lessons of his folly. Yet there are limitations to their rationalism. Both become slaves to passion for Edmund. We see, says Heilman, that they are truly "Centaurs: we see rational mind unmistakably in conjunction with, and in the service of, animal body." In the end, the alliance between the sisters breaks up and each "goes her own rational way." In the end both are destroyed because "they have lacked the power of imagination by which they might have got hold of disciplinary, saving values."

Associated with the sisters is Edmund, who proclaims his rationality in his opening soliloquy. He argues that as a bastard may be as handsome and noble as a legitimate child; he plans to live by his wits and to snatch Edgar's inheritance from him. (Heilman notes in passing that Edmund is really finding a rational justification for doing what he emotionally wants to do.) His kind of rationalism appears again in his betrayal of his father to Cornwall. However, "with Edmund as with the sisters, the rational presentation of advantage ironically falls down when the complexity of experience becomes too much for it . . . it not only wantonly injures others but ruins the basis of human order; it destroys the soul of its practitioner." Edmund at the end of the play has become ineffectual. Heilman concludes from an examination of these three characters, and from a shorter examination of Oswald and Cornwall, that "reason is insufficient" to manage the complexities of human experience.

Heilman also distinguishes a number of thematic and meta-phorical patterns in the play. For example, in Chapter II, he singles out "the sight pattern" at the beginning of the play. Gloucester is lacking in insight and so does not see through Edmund's plot and fails to take significant action when Cornwall puts Kent in the stocks. He is "tragically slow in seeing what is implied in the situations in which he finds himself." His blinding by Cornwall, then, is "an ironic comple-tion of his career." He rightfully says "I stumbled when I saw." Yet after his blinding he does, ironically, see the truth, that Edgar whom he mistrusted is loyal to him. "The blinding of Gloucester is at once an act of vengeance by the tyrant, an expiatory suffering by Gloucester, and an ironic commentary on human experience."

In Chapter III, "Poor Naked Wretches," Heilman examines "the clothes pattern," which he thinks illuminates the contrast between appearance and reality. Edgar, for example, who is nearly naked, is clothed only in a blanket in the storm scene. His nakedness is a symbol of his "defenselessness in the world." Yet at the same time, paradoxically, it serves as a defense for him. As for Lear, several references to dress prepare us for the scene where Lear tears off his clothes to become himself a poor naked wretch. He "divests" himself of rule; "raiment is a symbol of what he has given us"; he runs into the storm "unbonneted." Eventually he recognizes the sufferings of "poor naked wretches" whose "houseless heads" he now begins to pity. He learns that "unaccommodated man is no more but . . . a poor, bare forked animal." Reference to crown and head are also seen as significant. "In Act I Lear took off a crown; in Act III he was bareheaded; and now he has a mock crown"—the fantastic garb of flowers in Act IV. "In one sense, Lear has his crown of thorns." Heilman also sees significance in the "fresh garments" which are put on him while he sleeps. "Lear gets a fresh start." Finally, Lear "having thrown away clothes which have no meaning," comes to his last rest and dies. "The king's only safe divestment is death."

Heilman also has chapters on Nature in *Lear* (Ch. V) and a consideration of the justice of the gods (Ch. X).

W. R. Keast, in a long article "The 'New Criticism' and *King Lear*" (1949; reprinted 1952) takes issue with Heilman's work. His main quarrel is with what he deems the overemphasis on imagery and insufficient emphasis on plot, character, and thought. He notes the recurrent images which are studied by Heilman: the "sight pattern," "the madness pattern," the "values pattern," the clothes imagery, the animal imagery, the references to nature and age, "the justice pattern," and the "religion pattern." He notes that Heilman tries to relate all these constituent metaphors "to the large metaphor which is the play itself." He criticizes Heilman for assuming that the plot is the least important element in the play, the one which expresses its meaning least completely, while "the structure can be set forth only by means of its patterns of imagery." The characters, too, Keast claims, are neglected in favor of the imagery. "The primary sources and guaranty of the symbolic values he attaches to elements of the play are not in his inductions from the evidence of the text but in the necessities of his own theories of tragedy and morality." Frequently the symbolism claimed by Heilman contradicts "the plain meaning of the text." For example, in the scene where Gloucester demands to see the supposed letter from Edgar, Heilman detects an irony in the fact that, when Gloucester "most fails to see where he is going, he feels, like Oedipus, most shrewd and observant." The sight pattern "points the issue for us," as Gloucester three times repeats "Let's see." Keast takes issue with this: "But it is obvious that when Gloucester asks to see the letter, he does not feel shrewd and observant . . . he feels the impatience of a curious and interested man when teased." In any case, since we do not know yet whether Gloucester will be deceived, we are not in a position to observe any irony in his remarks. Further, in his attempts to find in Shakespeare's references to physical darkness symbolic references to Gloucester's blindness about his sons, Heilman forces the language beyond common sense. It is clear to Keast that the references to night (in II, 1) are there because the scene takes place at night and because Shakespeare, whose plays were often performed in the daylight, had to establish that fact. Keast finds "the same arbitrariness" in assigning symbolic values in other parts of Heilman's discussion. He complains, too, that when Heilman "attempts to justify his symbolic readings by showing their superiority over other readings" he is again arbitrary in that he chooses alternatives which are "unlikely or absurd." He usually does not say whose the alternate reading is, but merely sets it up as inferior to his own. Keast points out that Heilman's case would be strengthened if he chose reputable interpretations to compete with his own. Keast further questions Heilman's generalization that "Shakespeare had got hold of the modern problem, which he assumes to be the conflict between the old order and the new" (the latter symbolized by Goneril). He thinks "the" modern problem is not so easy to identify and wonders why Goneril in particular should symbolize the new order.

Heilman's conception of imagery makes the play sound as if it were "an inferior philosophic dialogue," with its oversimplifications and "very simple dichotomies." If imagery is to be meaningful, it must find its meaning in the characters and situations of the drama. In short, "Heilman has deprived himself of the one principle of order among his patterns—the artistic order provided by the plot of *King Lear*."

Divergent attitudes to the final meaning of *King Lear* are found in Judah Stampfer's "The Catharsis of *King Lear*" (1960) and Oscar James Campbell in his essay on the play in *The Living Shakespeare*. Stampfer reminds us that Shakespeare imposed a tragic ending on a story that ended happily in its sources. He remarks, "Part of the poignance of *King Lear* lies in the fact that its issues, and the varieties of evil that it fuses are so central to Christianity, while it is denied any of the mitigation offered by a well defined heaven and hell, and a formal doctrine of supernatural salvation." Bradley found some sense of reconciliation at the end of the play in that he interprets Lear's last speech ("Look on her, look, her lips / Look there, look there") as an indication that Lear thought Cordelia was alive and that he died in an ecstasy of joy. If this is not so, Stampfer points out, the universe is one (as indicated in Lear's previous speech) "in which dogs, horses, and rats live and Cordelias are butchered." Stampfer thinks the textual evidence of the final lines of the plays shows that Lear did not die of joy, but in the knowledge that Cordelia was dead. This denouement, he concludes, "with the gratuitous, harrowing deaths of Cordelia and Lear, controverts any justice in the universe. Chance kills . . . the universe belongs to Edmund." The audience will recognize that the saintly life of Cordelia, the painful purgation of Lear, count for nothing. "And with Lear's death, each audience, by the ritual of the drama, shares and releases the most private and constricting fear to which mankind is subject, the fear that penance is impossible, that the covenant, once broken, can never be re-established, because its partner has no charity, resilience, or harmony— the fear, in other words, that we inhabit an imbecile universe. It is by this vision of reality that Lear lays down his life for his folly. Within its bounds lies the catharsis of Shakespeare's profoundist tragedy."

Campbell, on the other hand, tends to think of *Lear* as a "half-stoical, half-Christian" morality play "set against a backdrop of eternity." It depicts Lear's "agonized search and final discovery of the abiding spiritual values." When the play opens, Lear's values are not the true values. He is blinded by his love of luxury and pomp. According to Stoic thought, love of luxury was particularly objectionable in the old, and Lear has to learn through his suffering that the material things he has valued are unimportant compared with what matters most in the end, the Christian equivalent of Stoic peace, the love of Cordelia. Campbell finds the deaths of Lear and Cordelia in accordance with the tragic mood of the play. "It is the souls of the two that matter, and in their eternal union their souls are triumphant." Lear has been prepared by his suffering "not for life on this earth but for a Christian Heaven."

The German scholar Wolfgang Clemen (*The Development of Shakespeare's Imagery,* 1951), deals with images in the play. He notes that the language of Lear, the Fool, Edgar and Kent is rich in imagery, while Goneril, Regan and Edmund, who are cool, calculating and unimaginative people, who are not closely in touch with the elemental powers, are remarkable for the absence of imagery from their speech.

Imagery in the first act constantly points forward to future action. For example, Lear's seemingly hypocritical statement (for he is still strong and powerful) that he will "unburthen'd crawl toward death" points forward to the day when Lear will be reduced to the level of a hunted animal. Similarly Kent's "Kill thy physician, and the fee bestowe / Upon thy foul disease" looks forward to Lear's complaint to Goneril that she is "a disease that's in my flesh." France, when speaking of Cordelia, exclaims "Sure, her offence / Must be of such unnatural degree, / That monsters it." In the course of the play the word "monster" will frequently be applied to the unnatural behavior of the two other daughters.

The Fool's language is particularly rich in imagery. He often uses simple, everyday language to clarify the action. Thus he shows how by the simple simile of the two crowns of the divided egg Lear gave away his kingdom and power. Similarly he says, "Truth's a dog must to kennel; he must be whipped out," and "Shalt see thy other daughter will use thee kindly; for . . . she's as like this as a crab's like an apple," and (of Kent) "he wears cruel garters." "Horses are led by the heads, dogs and bears by the neck, monkeys by the loins, and men by the legs" shows that man fares no better than animals.

In the storm scene Clemen calls attention to the imperative "Crack nature's moulds, all germens spill at once, / That make ingrateful man." In the first act Lear had called on nature to make Goneril barren. Now he wants all nature, all mankind to be unfruitful. "To Lear's prophetic fantasy, the breaking of the natural bond between himself and his daughters, appears as a rent running through the whole of the universe. Just as human natures overstepped their boundaries . . . so do the elements now transcend their boundaries."

Jan Kott, in *Shakespeare: Our Contemporary* (1964) writes as a native of Poland (which has brilliantly alive theater) and an existentialist. He sees a similarity between tragedy—Lear in particular—and the theater of the grotesque. He goes so far as to see Edgar leading Gloucester over the cliff as an analogue of Beckett's *Endgame*. Beckett, he says, "eliminated all action, everything external, and repeated it in skeletal form." Both tragedy and the theater of the grotesque raise questions about justice, belief in the absolute, and hope for the solution of the conflict between a supposed moral order and daily life as it is lived. Tragedy is a theater of priests and the grotesque a theater of clowns. Kott believes that the clown is central in *Lear* as he goes with the King, Gloucester and Edgar into the storm. They are four madmen. Even the clown's language is close to the language of the grotesque. It uses "Biblical travesties and inverted medieval parables," "sudden leaps of imagination, condensations and epitomes, brutal, vulgar, and scatological expressions." He uses paradox and absurd humor. The clown disappears at the end of Act III. He is not needed anymore, for Lear himself has learned to speak the Fool's language.

Kott sees the theme of *Lear* as "the decay and fall of the world." First there is the proud court and its attendants, later only four beggars wandering in a storm. Lear loses not only his retainers and his kingdom, but also his identity as a king and a person. As early as the end of Act I, he says, "This is not

Lear. . . . Who is it that can tell me who I am?" But Lear's fate and (Kott implies) the fate of every man is not merely loss of position and identity. It is suffering. Lear will go mad, Kent will be humiliated and punished, Gloucester will lose his eyes and fall into despair. They are all maimed and tortured. At this point Kott compares *Lear* to *Endgame*. In the latter play Clov cannot sit down, the blind Hamm cannot get up. Nell and Nagg are almost dead in their trash cans. Clov reports that Nagg in his dustbin is crying. "Then he's living," comments Hamm. Similarly Lear comments:

> we came crying hither; . . . . When we are born, we cry
> that we are come / To this great stage of fools.

Like Nagg, Lear becomes "a ruin'd piece of nature."

The gods and the moral order and the possibility of justice probably do not exist; at any rate they do not manifest them-selves, any more than Godot comes (in Beckett's *Waiting for Godot*).

Men call on them, of course, sometimes by splendid Greek names, sometimes as "the gods." "But the gods do not inter-vene. They are silent. Gradually the tone becomes more and more ironical. The ruin of a man invoking God is ever more ridiculous." The characters also become ever more clownlike. Gloucester is plucked by the beard. Lear's prayers are "coun-tered by the Fool's scatological jokes," Gloucester's by "Edgar's clownish demonology," itself a travesty on "dream books and books on witchcraft; a great and brutal gibe." Both Hamm (in *Endgame*) and Lear realize that there is no justice and that fortune is blind. In Act IV Lear says:

> No rescue? What, a prisoner? I am ever / The natural
> fool of fortune.

"In a moment," comments Kott, "he will run off the stage.

Before that happens he will ask for his pinching shoe to be taken off. He is a clown now, so he can afford to do this . . . for clowns have performed the old medieval sotie [in medieval France, a short farcical play having allegorical figures] about the decay and fall of the world. But in both Shakespearean and Beckettian "Endgames" it is the modern world that fell; the Renaissance world, and ours."

ESSAY QUESTIONS AND ANSWERS

QUESTION

Discuss the religious attitudes displayed in *King Lear*.

ANSWER

King Lear takes place at a time when Britain was not yet fully under the influence of Christianity. Most of the people in the play, therefore, worship a set of pagan gods rather than the one God of Judeo-Christian tradition. The attitudes in the play range from Gloucester's superstition to Edmund's mocking disbelief in any supernatural forces. Gloucester believes that "These late eclipses in the sun and moon portend no good to us," and attributes the disinheriting of Cordelia in the first scene to supernatural heavenly interference. Edmund immediately mocks this attitude, singing "O, these eclipses do portend these divisions! fa, sol, la, mi." To Edmund man merely uses supernatural forces as an excuse for his own viciousness and folly. Gloucester's shallow faith is sorely tried in the scenes after his blinding. The gods are no longer kind and generous beings to him, but "As flies to wanton boys are we to the gods; / They kill us for their sport." Believing now that the gods are aggressively malignant, Gloucester wants to commit suicide, a symptom of utmost religious despair. He is prevented from doing so by his son, Edgar, who is the most devout male character in the play. Edgar believes that "The gods are just, and of our pleasant vices / Make instruments to plague us." In other words, there is a moral significance to what the gods do to us. The torment Gloucester has undergone has been just punishment for his moral laxity in begetting Edmund illegitimately. Edmund's attitude is simply, "Now, gods, stand up for bastards!" They seem to do so for a while, as Edmund's evil plot prospers, but ultimately he is destroyed by his own evil. The other characters in the play do not seem as much affected by religion as the Gloucester family. Lear is always praying to the "kind gods" to save him and punish his ungrateful daughters, but he feels that the universe is all awry, and when on rare occasions human beings behave well, "The gods themselves throw incense," and worship such saintlike people as Cordelia. With the noble, self-effacing character of Cordelia we have a figure who seems to embody the Christian ideal, and she is destroyed perhaps because she is one of the few really devout souls in an essentially cruel and irreligious world.

QUESTION
How does the Gloucester plot mirror the Lear plot?

ANSWER
King Lear is the only major Shakespearean tragedy in which a highly important subplot is interwoven with the main plot. This mingling of two plots goes far to account for the supreme richness and complexity of the play. Right from the first scene, the fortunes of the Gloucester family are compared with those of the Lear family, and as the play progresses, the two plots merge into one. Like Lear, Gloucester is an old widower who doesn't know enough about human nature to realize which of his children is good, which evil. Just as Goneril and Regan plot to reduce Lear to beggary, so Edmund schemes to get Edgar disinherited and Gloucester killed as a traitor. Just as Cordelia brings about Lear's spiritual redemption through her unselfish love, so Edgar saves his father from Edmund's plot, from Oswald's sword, and, ultimately, from suicide, by teaching him that "Men must endure / Their going hence, even as their coming hither: / Ripeness is all." Gloucester himself is aware of the similarity of his story to Lear's right from the beginning. In his speech about the "late eclipses in the sun and moon," he comments about Edgar, "This villain of mine comes under the prediction; there's son against father: the king falls from bias of nature, there's father against child." Throughout the play the Gloucester plot serves as a commentary on the Lear plot, and one enriches the other by showing that what happens in each is not unique, but the common fate of mankind.

QUESTION

What is the role of the Fool in the play, and why does he disappear so mysteriously?

ANSWER

In many ways the Fool is the most mysterious character in *King Lear*. He seems somehow outside the play because he never affects the action. Also, it is difficult to determine how old he is, or whether he is mad or sane, because the language he uses is complex, allusive and frequently archaic. His function in the court when Lear reigned was to entertain the King and court with his quips, puns, songs and riddles. Because he had no political power or social position, he was able to make sharp jokes at the expense of royalty and get away with them, as long as they were genuinely witty. Once Lear has abdicated, the Fool follows him about, although he resents the disinheriting of Cordelia, who was his favorite. It is the Fool's function in the play not merely to cheer up the King, but to teach him the extent of his folly. This he does with frequently cruel jokes. Thus he tells Lear, "thou madest thy daughters thy mother: for . . . thou gavest them the rod and puttest down thine own breeches." When Lear asks, "Dost thou call me fool, boy?" the Fool replies, "All thy other titles thou hast given away; that thou wast born with."

While the Fool is intensely loyal to Lear, he is not very brave. He is silent in the presence of Goneril and Regan and is terrified of the storm. Later he revives, but in Act III, Scene 6, he disappears with the strange words, "I'll go to bed at noon," which seems to indicate that he knows he is going to die soon. Then he is heard of no more, although at the end of the play Lear cries, "And my poor fool is hang'd!" This, however, refers to Cordelia, whom Lear calls "fool" as a term of affection. We never know what became of the Fool, but it is more likely that this is because Shakespeare felt he had already served his function than that he merely forgot about him. Once Lear has been made completely aware of his folly in dividing up the kingdom between Goneril and Regan and disinheriting Cordelia, the Fool is no longer necessary. An alternative reading of the role of the Fool suggests that in some sense, the Fool doubles for or replaces Cordelia: his remarks often point, at least, to Lear's great folly in disinheriting her, and he disappears from the play while Cordelia with France's army advances toward Britain. He is a constant reminder that goodness is still alive with Lear's youngest daughter.

QUESTION

Discuss the various aspects of madness in the play.

ANSWER

When Lear first realizes the extent of Goneril's ingratitude, he cries out, "O, let me not be mad, not mad, sweet heaven! / Keep me in temper: I would not be mad!" This prayer is repeated many times in the play, but nevertheless madness inexorably descends on the King. It takes many forms: the "trial" of Goneril and Regan in the hovel during the storm, the ineffectual curses on his daughters, the almost hysterical speech about sexual license in Act IV, Scene 6, and the wearing of flowers and weeds toward the end of the play. Lear's madness is more than the senility of the very old. It includes madness in the sense of bitter anger at the injustices of the world, and much of what Lear says when he is mad is very true and sane indeed. The anger of his madness reaches its peak during the storm; afterwards Lear is generally more subdued and almost childlike. It is almost as if Shakespeare were saying that in order to achieve a sane and balanced vision of a mad world, one must go mad oneself. Lear's madness is compared and contrasted in the storm scenes with the madness of the Fool and the pretended madness of Edgar. As the Fool says, "This cold night will turn us all to fools and madmen." The Fool is gibbering with terror and must be comforted by Kent. Edgar has taken the disguise of a harmlessly mad beggar with a religious persecution mania—he keeps seeing demons everywhere. Edgar's idea, of course, is that no one will suspect, or even take notice of Tom of Bedlam, the poor mad beggar, and so he will be safe from Edmund's plotting for the time being. In the storm scenes, King, Fool and beggar-noble are all reduced to the level of madness, but of varying degrees of intensity and purpose. Lear is brought to a calmer vision of his plight toward the end of the play by means of Cordelia's unvarying love, and the common-sense treatment of the physician, who realizes that the only "cure" for the King's condition is rest and loving care. The forces that drove him mad in the first place cannot be undone.

QUESTION

Is the brief, offstage battle scene an anticlimax after all the preparations for it during the play?

ANSWER

The political significance of the battle between the French and British armies must not be underestimated. Right from the beginning of the play a feud between Albany and Cornwall, each egged on by his ambitious wife, shows signs of breaking out into civil war. But the landing of the French army at Dover brings together Albany and Cornwall in an uneasy alliance. First the French must be defeated. They have landed because the King of France is married to Cordelia and wishes to restore Lear to the throne in Britain when he hears of how the old King has been mistreated. When Cornwall is killed by his servant, the British forces would seem to have suffered a defeat. But Edmund takes over Cornwall's army, backed by Regan, who loves him, and continues the march on Dover. Albany, however, had misgivings about the enterprise, because he has seen through his wife, who also loves Edmund, and has come to sympathize with Lear. Nevertheless, as a patriotic Englishman, he feels he must repel the French invasion.

There are three major reasons for the actual brevity of the

battle itself. First, none of the major characters involved is a soldier, so his behavior in battle is not significant or necessary for his portrayal as it is, say, in the history plays. Second, all that is important about the battle is its outcome—the capture of Lear and Cordelia by Edmund. And third, since the sympathies of Shakespeare's audience would be divided, like Albany's, between a desire to see justice done to Lear and Cordelia and a patriotic refusal to see the French win, Shakespeare probably thought it best to get the battle over with as quickly as possible. The play is very long as it is, and battle scenes on the scale of those in *Henry V* or *Antony and Cleopatra* would merely try the patience of the audience without making any significant contribution to the play.

QUESTION

In what respects is the concept of Nature as a beneficent ruling power observed and violated in the course of *King Lear*?

ANSWER

Closely associated with the belief in an ordered universe was the concept of Nature as a benign force in the universe. Nature in this sense is a principle of order linking all spheres of existence in their proper relationships. Of particular interest in connection with the play is her operation in connection with human relationships. By nature husband was bound to wife, child to parent, servant to master. In the play, Cordelia, Edgar and Kent all fulfill the demands of nature in this sense.

Although she has been deprived of her share of the kingdom, Cordelia remains loyal and loving toward her father. She seeks him out, heals him, loves him and comforts him. Similarly Edgar, although he has been slighted by Gloucester, acts toward him as a true son should, guiding him and saving him from despair. Kent also has been badly treated, dismissed unjustly from Lear's service. He remains a faithful, loyal follower, serving his master in disguise, and acting toward him always in gentleness and tenderness.

However, the rule of nature over human relationships can be violated and order in the universe disrupted. In the play, the affectional and moral relationships between members of families are disrupted by the unnatural actions of Edmund, Regan and Goneril. Edmund behaves unnaturally both toward his brother and his father. Disregarding the claims of primogeniture which were sanctioned by custom and order, he plots to gain Edgar's inheritance for himself by treachery. Toward his father also he is disloyal, deceiving and betraying him. His father remarks, "Our flesh and blood, my lord, is grown so vile, that it doth hate what gets it."

Goneril and Regan similarly violate the claims of child-parent relationships. When they are left alone at the end of the first scene, their cynicism about their father and their lack of real affection for him are clear. They see that he "hath ever but slenderly known himself," and they look for more "unconstant starts" in his behavior.

When Lear stays with Goneril, she deliberately picks a quarrel with her father, whose servants she finds a nuisance in her household. Ordering her steward Oswald to "put on what weary negligence you please," she plans to "breed . . . occasions" of quarrels with her father. She criticizes his knights as "disordered" and "debosh'd" and asks him to keep fewer retainers—fifty instead of a hundred. Lear turns to Regan and her husband Cornwall, who imprison Lear's servant Kent in the stocks, refuse to speak with him when he comes, and when they do come down, take Goneril's part, and say twenty-five followers are quite sufficient for Lear's needs. At the end of the scene, as the storm rises, they bar the gates of the castle against Lear, saying that his follies have asked for this treatment and that he needs a lesson. He is exposed to all the cruelty of the storm (Act III). When Albany finds out what they have done, he comments:

Humanity must perforce prey on itself, / Like monsters of the deep.

The sisters also violate the claims of marriage. Both lust after the bastard, Edmund. Their rivalry for him reaches its climax in the fifth act. Neither can bear to leave the other alone with him. In the end Goneril poisons Regan, and, when her treachery against her husband is discovered, kills herself. Both Regan and Goneril betray their father and their husbands, betray the claims of nature, and deserve the ends which come to them.

QUESTION
What comments on justice and injustice are made in the course of *King Lear*?

ANSWER
King Lear is permeated with comments on justice and injustice, though the play eventually grows beyond this concept.

Lear himself commits the initial acts of injustice. First, ignoring his responsibility as a king, he divides his kingdom. This is a great wrong to his country and results in civil war, as we shall see. Then, blind in his thirst for flattery to Cordelia's real goodness and affection, he banishes her from his kingdom. When Kent rightly tries to take her part, tries to show Lear that he is doing an act of injustice, Lear compounds his previous injustice by banishing Kent as well. Lear is to suffer himself as a result of these injustices.

In the next scene, as the subplot is initiated, we see Edmund similarly committing an act of injustice. He plans to deprive his older and legitimate brother of the heritage which was his according to the laws of nations. "Legitimate Edgar, I must have your land." Out of injustice, he plans to prosper, and succeeds in convincing his father of the lie that Edgar is plotting against his life.

The beginnings of the sisters' injustice appears in Scene 3, where Goneril orders Oswald to neglect her father: "Put on what weary negligence you please" and "Let his knights have colder looks among you." Oswald carries these orders out when next he sees Lear. Lear's sense of injustice at this treatment and at Goneril's proposal to deprive him of fifty of his men is expressed when he speaks of Goneril's ingratitude, "more hideous" than that of a sea monster. To him it is, "sharper than a serpent's tooth . . . to have a thankless child." He is beginning to feel injustice himself, but suffers still from that powerful egoism which he displayed in the opening scene. The first hint that Lear himself may overcome his egoism and develop a sense of justice comes at the very end of Act I, when the Fool is teasing him. Lear is not really listening, for suddenly he says "I did her wrong." He has realized how unjustly he treated Cordelia. We are soon to hear, also, that Lear's mistake in dividing the kingdom is causing civil war between Cornwall and Albany.

The theme of the injustice of Edmund to Edgar is resumed in the second act. Edmund persuades his father that Edgar attacked and wounded him, and succeeds in making his father swear to catch and punish Edgar and to reward Edmund: "Loyal and natural boy, I'll make thee capable" [i.e. of inheriting the estate]. Ironically, Edmund invokes the justice of "the revenging gods" of justice against his brother.

The next act of injustice is committed by Cornwall and Regan when they imprison Kent in the stocks, a punishment unfit, as Gloucester points out, for the King's messenger. When Lear discovers Kent in the stocks, he is outraged, and even more so when he discovers that Regan thinks he needs even fewer retainers than Goneril would allow: "What need you five and twenty, ten, or five?" asks Goneril. "What need one?" demands Regan. Here Lear argues for the claims of dignity, which go beyond the claims of justice: "Oh, reason not the need." He makes vows of revenge, at which Regan, invoking a kind of harsh justice, exclaims:

O sir, to wilfulness, / The injuries that they themselves procure / Must be their schoolmasters.

But she and Goneril, too, as well as Lear, will be punished for their injustice.

In the third act there is the first hint of retribution against Goneril and Regan and their husbands. Cordelia and the King of France are leading a power into England to rescue Lear from his enemies. Meanwhile, Lear challenges the storm to do its worst.

It cannot exceed the injustice of his daughters. Lear still seems to believe in justice, for he cries out, "Let the great gods, that keep this dreadful pother O'er our heads, / Find out their enemies now." He urges those who have committed "undivulged crimes" to tremble, the murderer, the perjured, the incestuous, and the false-seemer, to shake and cry for grace. He still feels he himself is a man "more sinned against than sinning." It is significant that now that he is unprotected in the face of this terrible storm, he feels the first stirrings of pity toward others weaker than himself. He wonders if the Fool is cold, and says, "I have one part in my heart / That's sorry for thee." This is followed (in Scene 4) by his recognition that he has not been concerned enough with the really poor and helpless of his kingdom.

Poor naked wretches, whereso'er you are, / That bide the beating of this pitiless storm / How shall your houseless heads and unfed sides, / Your loop'd and window'd raggedness, defend you / From seasons such as these? O I have ta'en / Too little care of this.

A little later, in a farm house on the heath, Lear once more reverts to his own sense of injustice. Calling his daughters she-foxes, he summons them to trial, making the Fool and the seeming madman (Edgar) act as their judges. This trial is another attempt, in a wild way, to seek justice, even through a travesty of conventional means. First he arraigns Goneril, saying "I here take my oath before this honorable assembly, she kicked the poor King her father." Then he tries Regan, commenting on her "warp'd looks," and complaining that there must be corruption in the courts, as she got away with her ill deeds. In his "anatomizing" of Regan, Lear asks the basic question about justice—"Is there any cause in nature that makes these hard hearts?" What is the true source of injustice? Edgar comments that his injustices now seem "light and portable" compared with Lear's. The "trial" of the two sisters in a way echoes the trial of the first scene (the love test) and foreshadows the trial in the next scene in which Cornwall unjustly tries Gloucester for treason, i.e. for being in touch with the French army and for trying to help Lear. Cornwall is quite aware that he is acting from a position of power, not of justice.

Pinion him like a thief, bring him before us. / Though well we may not pass upon his life / Without the form of justice, yet our power / Shall do a courtesy to our wrath, which men / May blame, but not control.

Urged on by the sisters, Cornwall plucks out both Gloucester's eyes. Such a "trial" is a travesty of justice and calls in question whether "the powers above" are just or not. It is perhaps fitting that at the moment when Gloucester suffers most from injustice, he also realizes his injustice to Edgar, for Regan tells him that it was Edmund who disclosed his "treason," and Gloucester exclaims "O my follies! Then Edgar was abused." He still believes in justice, for he swears "by the kind gods." It is interesting in this scene that even Cornwall's servants turn against their master. Shakespeare seems to say that even ordinary men, if pushed far enough, will take the side of justice.

In the fourth act Gloucester momentarily abandons his belief in the "kind gods," saying:

> As flies to wanton boys are we to the gods / They kill us for their sport.

But a few minutes later, after he meets the supposed madman (Edgar), he calls on the heavens to humble others as he has been humbled; so "distribution [i.e. distributive justice] should undo excess."

In the next scene a messenger brings to Albany the news of Cornwall's blinding of Gloucester and his (Cornwall's) death at the hands of his servant. Albany's comment is "This shows you are above, / You justicers, that these our nether crimes / So speedily can venge." He himself promises to revenge the loss of Gloucester's eyes. Not much is said about justice in the subsequent scenes, except that Gloucester twice prays to the gods, when he renounces the world in his attempted suicide and when he renounces the temptation to suicide. He calls them "mighty" and "gentle." It is implied that they have power over men. Justice gives way to mercy in the beautiful scene at the end of the act when Cordelia denies that the claims of "justice" against her father have any meaning for her. In her heart there is only forgiveness.

In the fifth act the action is wound up. Edgar comes to fight with Edmund, charging him with manifold treachery against the gods, his brother and his father. When Edmund falls, Edgar exclaims that "the gods are just." He reflects that his father's vice (i.e. in begetting Edmund illegitimately) cost him his eyes.

The deaths of Lear and Cordelia seem to some critics to be gratuitous and to indicate that the gods are not just. If Edmund had repented a few minutes earlier they could have been saved. Their deaths appear to depend merely on chance. Other critics feel that Lear and Cordelia have been prepared for a

Christian heaven, where Cordelia's virtue and Lear's newfound humility will be rewarded.

QUESTION

What imagery is used for Goneril and Regan in *King Lear* and what is its significance?

ANSWER

Goneril and Regan are often compared to animals. When Lear parts from Goneril at the end of Act I, after she has sneered at him and diminished the number of his retainers, he calls her a "detested kite," that is, a falconlike bird which preys on its quarry. He also compares her to "the sea-monster," by which he possibly means the hippopotamus, which had a reputation for ingratitude, or perhaps a mythological monster. Of her ingratitude he also remarks:

> How sharper than a serpent's tooth it is / To have a thankless child.

The Fool warns him that his other daughter will use him "kindly," that is with similar disfavor. Lear comments once more on his daughter's "monster ingratitude."

Lear seeks his other daughter, Regan, at Gloucester's castle, and finds that her husband has put his man (Kent) in the stocks and that both husband and wife have retired to bed and do not wish to see him. When Regan (who finally comes down) tells him he should be "ruled and led," Lear says that she "struck [him] with her tongue, / Most serpent-like, upon the very heart." He speaks of Goneril's "sharp-tooth'd unkindness, like a vulture," which pierced his heart. Both daughters seem to him now like unusually cruel animals. They show this when they shut him out into the stormy night.

In the storm scene, Lear's hurts from his daughters affect his attitude to the mad Tom of Bedlam (Edgar). He thinks, on the analogy of his own sufferings, that poor Tom must have been abused by his daughters. Nothing else could have brought him to such a pathetic state. "What, have his daughters brought him to this pass?" he asks. This reminds him of his own "pelican daughters"—an allusion to the medieval belief that pelican young fed on the blood of the parent bird. Gloucester sums up the situation which both of them are experiencing:

> Our flesh and blood is grown so vile, my lord, / That it doth hate what gets it.

Lear's sense of his daughter's ingratitude drives him to bring them to trial. He calls them "she-foxes," implying that they are cruel and vixenish. Later, when Gloucester upbraids Regan and Cornwall for their cruelty to Lear, he says he would not see Regan's cruel nails "pluck out his poor old eyes," nor Goneril "in his annointed flesh stick boarish fangs." He thinks of Goneril as one of the ugliest and fiercest of beasts.

The next comment on Goneril comes from Albany when he realizes how debased his wife really is. He calls the sisters "tigers, not daughters." When he thinks what the pair have done to their gracious, generous father, he concludes:

> Humanity must perforce prey on itself, / Like monsters of the deep.

A little later in this same scene, Goneril spits at her husband like a monstrous and disdainful cat. "Marry, your manhood, mew" (Daniel's emendation). In the next scene, Kent refers to the pair as Lear's "dog-hearted daughters."

In the great scene in which Lear and Gloucester meet at Dover, Lear makes an attack on all nature as adulterous and promiscuous. Once again he associates his daughters with unnatural behavior, with hypocritical women who appear to be chaste, but who are really as lustful as a fitchew (skunk;

supposed to be oversexed) or as a horse in spring. "Down from the waist they are but Centaurs," he concludes. He is right, at this juncture, for both Goneril and Regan are guilty of lust, both desiring the bastard Edmund as a lover. Edmund later comments that each of the sisters is as jealous of the other "as the stung / Are of the adder."

It will be noticed that most of the animals used in these comparisons are unpleasant—kite, serpent, vulture, pelican, fox, boar, tiger, cat, dog, fitchew, horse, adder—most of these have unattractive connotations. (Bradley concluded that Shakespeare did not think much of dogs!) Shakespeare is showing that the sisters are sinking from the level of man—who stood between the angels and the animals—to the level of the animals. They have become like some of the most unpleasant birds and animals of prey—the kite, the vulture, the fox, the tiger—and animals with ugly connotations such as the fitchew and the adder. In their cruelty and unnaturalness they are less than human.

SUBJECT BIBLIOGRAPHY AND GUIDE TO RESEARCH PAPERS

Any research paper on *King Lear* should first of all be based on a reliable, accurate text of the play with helpful notes. The best modern text is the New Arden Edition edited by Kenneth Muir and published by the Harvard University Press. A cheaper, more readily available edition which is also very good is the Pelican Shakespeare edition edited by Alfred Harbage and published in paperback by Penguin Books. A very handy edition which includes complete text, excerpts from the sources and from the major critics and an extensive bibliography is *King Lear: Text, Sources, Criticism,* edited by G. B. Harrison and Robert F. McDonnel, and published in paperback by Harcourt, Brace & World. A good, more recent text is The *Complete Signet Classic Shakespeare* (edited by Sylvan Barnet, New York: Harcourt, 1972.)

Critical books and articles on *King Lear* abound. The following is a highly selective list of the most important *Lear* criticism, arranged alphabetically by author within key research topics:

BIBLIOGRAPHY
Champion, Larry S. *King Lear: An Annotated Bibliography.* 2 vols. New York: Garland, 1980.

Gaskell, Philip. *A New Introduction to Bibliography.* New York: Oxford University Press, 1972.

GENERAL STUDIES OF SHAKESPEARE'S LEAR
Alderman, Janet. *Twentieth-Century Interpretations of* King Lear. Englewood Cliffs: Prentice Hall, 1978.

Halliday, F. E. *A Shakespeare Companion.* Rev. ed., 1964. Baltimore: Penguin, 1969.

Ray, Robert H., ed. *Approaches to Teaching Shakespeare's* King Lear. New York: The Modern Language Association of America, 1986. Presents information on materials and references as well as critical essays on the play.

SHAKESPEARE'S USE OF HIS SOURCES
Questions to consider: What were the sources for *King Lear?* How do we know which of them Shakespeare had read? How did he alter them to suit his own purposes?

Greg, W. W., "The Date of *King Lear* and Shakespeare's Use of Earlier Versions of the Story," *The Library,* 4th Series, XX (1939–40), pp. 377–400.

Law, Robert Adger, "Holinshed's Lear Story and Shakespeare's," *Studies in Philology,* Vol. 47 (1950), pp. 42–50.

Leggatt, Alexander. *Twayne's New Critical Introductions to Shakespeare:* King Lear. Boston: Twayne Publishers, 1988. "By examining Shakespeare's revisions and tracing their implications for performance of the play, Leggatt reveals the extent to which the theatrical qualities that have been lost in the traditional conflated text offer new insights into both characterization and theme."

Muir, Kenneth, *Introduction to The New Arden* King Lear. Cambridge: Harvard University Press, 1952.

Perkinson, R. H., "Shakespeare's Revision of the Lear Story and the Structure of *King Lear,*" *Philological Quarterly,* Vol. 22 (1943), pp. 315–29.

Taylor, Gary and Michael Warren. *The Division of the Kingdoms: Shakespeare's Two Versions of* King Lear. Oxford Shakespeare Studies. Oxford: Clarendon Press, 1983.

Twelve commissioned essays on scholarship and literary criticism and an index of passages; the thesis is that the Quarto and the Folio texts are two independent versions of *Lear* which should not be combined.

RELIGIOUS AND ETHICAL BACKGROUND

Questions to consider: What is the overall religious meaning of *King Lear*? Is it Christian, pagan, stoic, agnostic, atheist? What was Shakespeare's conception of pre-Christian Britain? What is considered ethical, what unethical about the behavior of specific characters in the play? What does Edmund mean when he says Nature is his "goddess"?

Bald, R. C., "Thou Nature Art My Goddess: Edmund and Renaissance Free Thought," *Joseph Quincy Adams Memorial Studies*. Ithaca: Cornell University Press, 1948, pp. 337–49.

Craig, Harden, "The Ethics of *King Lear,*" *Philological Quarterly,* Vol. 4 (1925), pp. 97–109.

Danby, John F. *Shakespeare's Doctrine of Nature: A Study of* 'King Lear.' London: Faber, 1949.

Elton, William. King Lear *and the Gods*. San Marino: Huntington Library, 1960.

Goldberg, S. L. *An Essay on* King Lear. Cambridge: Cambridge University Press, 1974. The critic sees the play in moral terms and says that it is an appeal to the reader's feeling about natural justice. Goldberg follows the internal logic of the play and, he says, so avoids the pitfalls of doctrinaire literary interpretations.

Heilman, Robert B., "The Lear World," *English Institute Essays, 1947,* New York: Columbia University Press, 1948, and "The Two Natures in *King Lear,*" *Accent,* Vol. 8 (1947), pp. 51–59.

Parr, Johnstone, "Edmund's Nativity in *King Lear*" and "The 'Late Eclipses' in *King Lear*," *Tamburlaine's Malady and Other Essays,* Tuscaloosa: University of Alabama Press, 1953.

Ribner, Irving, "The Gods Are Just: A Reading of *King Lear*," *Tulane Drama Review,* Vol. 2 (1958), pp. 34–54.

Rinehart, Keith, "The Moral Background of *King Lear*," *University of Kansas Review,* Vol. 20 (1954), pp. 223–38.

Tillyard, E. M. W. *The Elizabethan World Picture.* London: Chatto & Windus, 1943. Although this book is not specifically about *Lear,* it is the classic statement on Elizabethan ideas about order in the cosmos and the dangers of upsetting the natural scheme of things.

THE POLITICAL AND HISTORICAL BACKGROUND

Questions to consider: What are the politics of *King Lear*? How would the Elizabethan audience react to the power struggle between Edmund, Albany and Cornwall? To the French invasion? What does Lear's abdication do to the political structure of Britain? Are the political assumptions in the play similar to those in Shakespeare's other tragedies? To those of the chronicle history plays?

Aers, David, and Gunther Kress. "The Language of Social Order: Individual, Society, and Historical Process in *King Lear*," *Literature, Language, and Society in England: 1580–1680.* Editors: David Aers, Bob Hodge, and Gunther Kress. Dublin: Gill, 1981.

Greg, W. W., "Time, Place and Politics in *King Lear*," *Modern Language Review,* Vol. 35 (1940), pp. 431–46.

Muir, Edwin, "The Politics of *King Lear*," *Essays on Literature and Society,* London: Hogarth Press, 1949.

Murphy, John L. *Darkness and Devils: Exorcism and* King Lear. Ohio: Ohio University Press, 1984. "Murphy explains the detailed connections between the English Papist exorcisings of the mid 1580s, 'The Babington Plot,' the trial and execution of Mary Queen of Scots, and Harsnett's satire as they relate to the world of *King Lear.*"

THE STORM SCENES

Questions to consider: How were the storm scenes staged in Shakespeare's day? To what extent are they symbolic of the inner storm in Lear's mind? Of general disorder in Nature?

Dunn, E. Catherine, "The Storm in *King Lear,*" *Shakespeare Quarterly,* Vol. 3 (1952), pp. 329–33.

Williams, G. W., "The Poetry of the Storm in *King Lear,*" *Shakespeare Quarterly,* Vol. 2 (1951), pp. 57–71.

LEAR'S FOLLY AND MADNESS

Questions to consider: How does the tragedy arise from Lear's character? Is Lear senile or insane in the first scene? What is the progress of his madness through the play? What were Elizabethan assumptions about madness and its treatment? Is Lear like other "mad" characters in the play (Edgar and the Fool)? Is his madness like Hamlet's?

Ashton, J. W., "The Wrath of King Lear," *Journal of English and Germanic Philology,* Vol. 31 (1932), pp. 530–36.

Campbell, Lily B. *Shakespeare's Tragic Heroes: Slaves of Passion.* New York: Barnes & Noble, 1959. Paperback.

Kahn, Sholom J., "'Enter Lear Mad,'" *Shakespeare Quarterly* Vol. 8 (1957), pp. 311–29.

Maclean, Norman, "Episode, Scene, Speech and Word: The Madness of Lear," *Critics and Criticism* (ed. R. S. Crane), Chicago: University of Chicago Press, 1952.

Muir, Kenneth, "Madness in *King Lear*," *Shakespeare Survey* (ed. Allardyce Nicoll), Cambridge: Cambridge University Press, 1960. Vol. XIII contains many other articles on *King Lear*.

SIGNIFICANCE OF THE FOOL

Questions to consider: What was the traditional place of the fool, or jester in court? Is Shakespeare's Fool typical? Is he young or old? What does he teach Lear? Is the Fool really mad? Why does he drop out of the play so mysteriously?

Empson, William, "Fool in *Lear*," *The Structure of Complex Words,* New York: New Directions, 1951.

Goldsmith, Robert H. *Wise Fools in Shakespeare*. East Lansing: Michigan State University Press, 1955.

Welsford, Enid. *The Fool*. New York: Doubleday Anchor, 1961. Paperback. The definitive work on the subject.

THE GLOUCESTER PLOT

Questions to consider: Why does Shakespeare use a subplot in *Lear*? How does Gloucester's story parallel Lear's? Why does Edmund hate his father so much? What is the attitude of characters in the play to Gloucester's superstition? How does blindness affect Gloucester?

Kreider, P. V., "Gloucester's Eyes," *Shakespeare Association Bulletin,* Vol. 8 (1933), pp. 121–32.

Stewart, J. I. M., "The Blinding of Gloster," *Review of English Studies,* Vol. 21 (1945), pp. 264–70.

Stoll, E. E., "Kent and Gloster," *Life and Letters,* Vol. 9 (1933), pp. 431–45.

IMAGERY

Questions to consider: How does Shakespeare use similes and metaphors to bring out the meaning of the play? Why all the animal images? Why the references to clothing and nakedness? (Lear's last words are "Pray you, undo this button.") Why all the images of sight and blindness?

Clemen, Wolfgang H. *The Development of Shakespeare's Imagery*. London: Methuen & Co., 1951.

Greenfield, Thelma N., "The Clothing Motif in *King Lear,*" *Shakespeare Quarterly,* Vol. 5 (1954), pp. 281–86.

Keast, William R., "Imagery and Meaning in the Interpretation of *King Lear,*" *Critics and Criticism* (ed. R. S. Crane), Chicago: University of Chicago Press, 1952.